German racer Hans Stuck demonstrates the driving prowess that led to his
unofficial title as "king of the mountains" in the painting by Walter Gotschke on
the cover. Driving a three-liter Austro-Daimler for four years, from
1927 to 1931, Stuck secured forty-six hill climb wins, forty f.t.d.
awards and was twice Austrian and once Swiss hill climb champion. The Gotschke
painting is an indication of what will be in store for race enthusiasts
when the artist completes his series of paintings of great cars, great drivers
and great races of the decades from the Twenties through the Sixties. Certain to be
included in the series on the Forties will be the cars of Tony Lago.
The Lago crest is debossed on the back cover.

automobile
Quarterly

THE CONNOISSEUR'S MAGAZINE OF MOTORING TODAY, YESTERDAY AND TOMORROW

SPRING/SUMMER 1965   VOLUME IV, NUMBER 1

LIMITED EDITION

EDITOR AND PUBLISHER:
L. SCOTT BAILEY

MANAGING EDITOR:
MERVYN KAUFMAN

ASSOCIATE EDITOR:
BEVERLY RAE KIMES

DESIGNER:
DALE WEAVER TOTTEN

EDITORIAL ASSISTANTS:
MARGARET T. BAILEY, GISELE SIMON

RESEARCH ASSOCIATES:
HENRY AUSTIN CLARK, JR., U.S.A.;
JACQUES ROUSSEAU, FRANCE;
MICHAEL SEDGWICK, GREAT BRITAIN;
NICOLÁS FRANCO, JR., SPAIN

CONTRIBUTING EDITORS:
ROBERT F. ANDREWS, CHARLES L. BETTS, JR.,
JOHN BOND, CHARLES DOLLFUS, ARTHUR W. EINSTEIN, JR.

LESLIE R. HENRY, DIETER KORP,
DENISE MCCLUGGAGE, JAN P. NORBYE,
D. CAMERON PECK, KEN W. PURDY, GIANNI ROGLIATTI,
RALPH STEIN, CARL L. WAGNER

ARTISTS:
JEROME D. BIEDERMAN, WALTER GOTSCHKE, P. W. M. GRIFFIN,
PETER HELCK, PAUL HØYRUP, LESLIE SAALBURG

PHOTOGRAPHERS:
HORST H. BAUMANN, GIORGIO BELLIA, TOM BURNSIDE,
IRVING DOLIN, ALEXANDRE GEORGES, ROBERT S. GRIER,
DAN RUBIN, JULIUS WEITMANN, NORMAN WILLOCK

PRODUCTION MANAGER:
CHESTER R. DETURK

CIRCULATION MANAGER:
JOHN HEFFELFINGER

ASSISTANT CIRCULATION MANAGER:
JEAN FREDERICK

BUSINESS MANAGER:
JACOB R. ESSER

AUTOMOBILE *Quarterly* IS PUBLISHED QUARTERLY BY AUTOMOBILE *Quarterly*, INC., EDITORIAL OFFICES: 515 MADISON AVENUE, NEW YORK, N. Y. 10022. TELEPHONE: PLAZA 8-2374. OFFICE OF PUBLICATION: 245 WEST MAIN STREET, KUTZTOWN, PENNSYLVANIA 19530. TELEPHONE: 683-7341. AUTOMOBILE *Quarterly* IS PRINTED IN THE UNITED STATES BY THE KUTZTOWN PUBLISHING COMPANY; COLOR SEPARATIONS BY LITHO-ART, INC., NEW YORK CITY; BINDING BY NATIONAL PUBLISHING COMPANY, PHILADELPHIA, PENNSYLVANIA. SINGLE COPIES: $5.95; ANNUAL SUBSCRIPTIONS: $21.00 IN U. S., $22.00 ELSEWHERE. ALL SUBSCRIPTIONS, ORDERS, CHANGES OF ADDRESS AND CORRESPONDENCE CONCERNING SUBSCRIPTIONS SHOULD BE SENT TO 245 WEST MAIN STREET, KUTZTOWN, PENNSYLVANIA 19530. SECOND-CLASS POSTAGE PAID AT KUTZTOWN, PENNSYLVANIA, AND AT ADDITIONAL MAILING OFFICES.

CONTENTS

The New Ford Station Wagon

ILLUSTRATION FROM AN ADVERTISEMENT APPEARING IN
THE SPORTSMAN, JUNE, 1929.

THE CARS OF TONY LAGO

collection: VOJTA F. MASHEK

photography: TOM BURNSIDE

4

Their ancestry goes back to the Nineteenth Century and proceeds from there in a maze of begetting on both sides of the channel: Darracq, Clément-Bayard, Clément, Clément Talbot, Talbot—and finally in 1920 the Sunbeam-Talbot-Darracq empire with factories in Wolverhampton, England, and Suresnes, France. Within fifteen years the STD combine was to break up, with the Rootes Group acquiring Wolverhampton and British rights in the name of Sunbeam and Talbot, and Major Antony Lago taking over the Suresnes branch with rights in the name of Talbot and Darracq.

From 1936 to 1958 the automobiles built in Suresnes came to be variously identified as Talbot-Lagos in France, as Talbot-Darracqs in Belgium and Luxembourg and as Darracqs in England, the latter designation used to distinguish them from the English Talbots. That some of this confusion was felt in the parent organization is evidenced by a postwar Suresnes brochure: following the opening page with its notation "manufactured by Automobiles Darracq-Talbot S.A." is the foreword which advises, "To avoid confusion, cars exported in certain Countries by Automobiles Talbot S.A. (sic) are now known as 'Lago.'" Those unnamed countries, from all available information, excluded the above mentioned nations, as well as all French possessions, Switzerland, Italy and Spain. Such genealogy makes one cry for the truth of Coleridge's "what are names but air" and decide the easiest way out is simply to designate Suresnes automobiles from 1936 to 1958 as the cars that Tony Lago built.

Major Antony Lago himself presents somewhat of an enigma. His long association with the automobile industry in France has led more than a few writers to assume he was French. Actually he was an Italian, born in Venice in 1893 and educated at the Turin school of engineering. His rank of major in the Italian army reserve was the result of successive promotions as an army officer during the First World War. At the war's end he left Italy; years later he would take France as his adopted country. Yet he served his native land as president of the Italian chamber of commerce in Paris after World War II, and his will stipulated that upon his death he was to be buried in Italy.

His friends were legion—in Italy, in France and in England where he received his first taste of the excitement of the automobile world. He began initially by selling Isotta-Fraschinis in London. In 1923 he joined Lap Engineering of London as technical director, and two years later secured a similar position with the Wilson company, for whom he assisted in perfecting the Wilson self-changing gearbox. Two years later he became associated with Armstrong-Siddeley, acquired the foreign selling rights to the Wilson gearbox from Sir John Siddeley, and drove with the works team in the 1932 Alpine Trials. That same year he was engaged by the English branch (Sunbeam-Talbot) of the STD combine as assistant director. By this time Tony Lago's attraction to the automobile had become almost mesmeric, and his spirit was indefatigable. The condition of the STD organization on either side of the channel, however, was far from healthy. In 1933, after the board of directors in London assessed the French situation as more critical, they dispatched Lago to the Suresnes branch with the hope of transfusing new blood into that ailing operation. It has been variously reported that during the STD era, the British hand, with the exception of yearly financial statements, never knew what its French hand was doing. In any event, when the breakup came, Antony Lago was the natural heir to the doddering organization in Suresnes. He resigned his Wolverhampton position and took over control of Société Anonyme Darracq cum Automobiles Talbot.

A quick glance around him was all Lago needed to assure himself that what he owned was almost a corpse. The products of Suresnes—one of France's and the world's oldest automobile manufacturing plants—were viewed with apathy by both the French car-buying public and the company personnel. Nonetheless Major Lago plunged into his work with characteristic elan. His approach to the Talbot problem was perhaps obvious but it was one that could have spelled immediate disaster. Speed and luxury were his guide lines, and racing—regardless of the contemporary rigorous competition—was his goal. Within eighteen months the old apathy was to be replaced by pride and interest.

Lago had an excellent base from which to work, the Talbot-Darracq three-liter Type K78 with a seven main-bearing, six-cylinder engine and in-line pushrod-operated overhead valves. A special high-performance cylinder head for that engine was developed by Lago and built to the designs of his chief engineer Walter Becchia. Its unorthodox and ingenious feature was the valve-gear that used cross-pushrods of unequal length, thus providing a relatively inexpensive and uncomplicated hemispherical head layout. As such it was patented by Lago. In competition two-Solex-carburetor form, output of the Lago Special powerplant was 165 bhp at 4,200 rpm. The car's chassis was similar to that of the Delahaye—a rugged, heavy construction with solid rear axle and independent front suspension by transverse leaf and A-arms. And, of course, the Lago car utilized the combination friction clutch and Wilson preselector gearbox operable with one pedal.

With his four-liter cars completed, Major Lago was ready to go racing. To him, racing was not only his finest laboratory, but his most effective sales campaign as well. Were neither of those factors to be considered, Antony Lago would have raced nonetheless—raced for the sport of it, for

At left and on preceding page is a 1939 two-place teardrop coupé, Type 150C-SS, with Pourtout coachwork. Its four-liter engine (90 x 104.5 mm) develops 140 hp at a recommended 4,100 rpm. Top speed is 128 mph.

the thrill of racing was his all-consuming passion. With gusto and perhaps a bit of presumption, he journeyed to Italy and persuaded champion driver René Dreyfus, then with Ferrari, to join and manage the Lago team in its debut racing year.

During that first year, the Lago team was largely held together by speculation. The Lago engine: would it last? Almost everyone, including Major Lago, feared it wouldn't. Nonetheless with the dawning of June's last Sunday in 1936, the Lago cars—in racing these came to be known as Talbots, Talbot-Lagos or Lago-Talbots—were being readied for the French Grand Prix at Montlhéry. After a frank appraisal that the car probably wouldn't be able to last the race, Major Lago advised Dreyfus, "Your job will be to stay ahead of the Bugattis for as long as you can. That's all I want." And he got it. After hanging onto the Bugattis for a respectable distance, Dreyfus's car ended the race with a noticeable limp. The final result did not daunt Major Lago—the three Lago cars finished eighth, ninth and tenth—he would remember only a few glorious laps. And the picture was to brighten the following year as Lago's cars finished the French Grand Prix first, second, third and fifth. Then there was the Tourist Trophy at Donington where Gianfranco Comotti and René Lebegue drove in one-two across the finish line. Raymond Sommer gave Lago's cars a first in both the Marseilles and the Tunis GP.

According to magazine reports of the Paris Salon that year, the Talbot-Lago exhibit virtually shone with the sweet glow of success. And well it might, for the same engine that made a place for Lago in the world of racing was also being used in Gran Turismo cars with rakishly unorthodox and beautiful bodies and a touring speed of about 118 mph. The Lago automobile was soon to be dubbed the "car that beguiles." And beguiling it was in either the production or the racing version. The fact that most cars competing on the circuits bore little or no resemblance to production models of the same marque was abhorrent to Lago. Lago wanted racing winners, to be sure, but he wanted his winning cars to use as many production parts as possible. That virtually every Lago automobile was race-bred was a source of pride to him.

In 1938 Lago bored out the engine of his competition car to 4½ liters (240 bhp) and mounted it in a quasi-Grand Prix car. The only major changes in chassis layout were the offset mounting of the powerplant to provide a low seating position and independent front suspension by A-arms. By adding or taking away fenders and other road equipment to meet various racing requirements, the car could be run in both sports and Grand Prix events. There has been, in fact, some dispute as to whether this

Coachwork by Figoni et Falaschi on a 1937 Type 150-SS two-place cabriolet with spine down trunk. The car has a regular chassis, but is equipped for competition, which means a dual braking system and higher compression. 9

unsupercharged 4½-liter machine was a thinly disguised GP machine or merely a "converted" sports car. As a GP car, despite its reliability and light fuel consumption, it was of course no match for the German brutes. This was evident in 1938, and the same engine modified the following year with power output raised to 250 bhp at 5,000 rpm did not bring the car any closer to the Grand Prix masters. The two Lago cars entered in the 1939 French Grand Prix finished third and fourth, albeit many miles behind the winning Auto-Unions.

On September 3, 1939, France declared war on Germany, and everything changed. Prior to the declaration Major Lago had created, under the name of Société Anonyme Française Talbot Darracq, a company for the manufacture of aircraft engines, and with the outbreak of hostilities he equipped his Suresnes factory for production of Pratt and Whitney power units. After the collapse of France, of course, war production ceased, and the factory shut down. Antony Lago's Italian nationality prevented the Germans from seizing the plant.

The war did not entirely still the engines of Lago's competition machines, however. The two cars built for the 1939 French GP were bought by racing drivers René Lebegue and Jean Trévoux. Early in 1941 the cars were smuggled out of France by way of Spain and put aboard a steamer bound for the United States and the Indianapolis 500. The cars unfortunately failed to qualify at Indy, but Lebegue and Trévoux proceeded west, later in the year attaining third and fourth f.t.d. in the Pike's Peak Hill Climb.

With the war over, Lago determined to pick up just where he had left off in 1939 and brought out from retirement his experimental 4½-liter engine. Among other improvements, its single camshaft was replaced by two camshafts set high in the block. The inclined valves were worked through short pushrods and rockers, thus greatly reducing the weight of the valve gear and providing more efficient action. This engine—the largest passenger car powerplant then built in France—provided the power for both standard and racing cars. Their channel-section chassis frames featured independent front suspension by transverse leaf spring and a hollow upper wishbone, and a one-piece rear axle mounted on semi-elliptic leaf springs. In the Grand Prix cars, the transmission was stepped to the right so that it ran alongside the driving seat to an offset differential assembly. In Grand Sport form the engines were mounted in a longer, heavier chassis; with regular coachwork, a speed of 125 mph was claimed. In each of these versions the Wilson gearbox was standard equipment.

There has been considerable controversy over the Wilson gearbox; that it is terrifying, difficult to adjust and hard to handle is the general im-

The 1950 Grand Sport, a two-place grand touring coupé with coachwork by Pennock of the Hague. Its six-cylinder engine (93 x 110 mm) develops 160 bhp at 4,000 rpm. Carburetion is through two Stromberg carburetors.

pression. Heavy traffic does not, of course, provide ideal conditions for its operation. Positive positioning of the preselector steering column lever on its quadrant is most important, but once this skill has been mastered, there is no mystery. The box is less fierce than demanding—it must be treated with respect. Once the car is under way, the lever in any gear can be positioned, preparatory, for example, to fast cornering. Nothing will happen until the driver judges that the selected gear should be engaged; then, a quick "punch" on the clutch-pedal and the engine revs take over. Properly adjusted, therefore, the Wilson was an ideal racing box—and so rugged, so the legend goes, that in the event of brake failure in fast competition, the box could be thrown into reverse, effectively stopping the car without blowing up the box.

Whether such was the case is a moot point. Undeniable is the fact that after the war Lago competition cars with the Wilson box became headline material in the racing press. The competition, of course, was considerably less formidable than in the prewar years, and this accounts for much of the Lago success. But success viewed from any angle is impressive. First-place finishes in five Grands Prix—including the thirty-fourth running of the French GP—and the Coupe du Salon in 1947 was a healthy beginning. Then there were six racing firsts in 1948, five in 1949 and ten in 1950. Among these, the 1950 win at Le Mans saw the Lago car driven by Louis Rosier and his son break every course record.

It was not that the Lago cars were fast; their 240 bhp was not really a match for the supercharged 1½-liter Alfa Romeos, Ferraris and Maseratis. But a nine-mile-per-gallon running consumption made them two or three times less thirsty than the Italians, and the ability to run through a Grand Prix nonstop was a decided advantage. The temperate tortoise often waited at the finish line for the hare.

"When one of my cars wins a race," Tony Lago is reported to have said, "I feel that I am paying a moral debt to the country which has permitted me to realize my life's dream." Unfortunately it was to be an all too short dream. The cars Lago placed on the circuits were largely the same automobiles he placed on the road. And the postwar French taxation system was not favorable to builders of luxurious grand touring cars.

Lago's Grand Sport was just that—a sports car in the grand manner. With gracefully swept and daringly distinctive coachwork by Saoutchik, Figoni et Falaschi and Pourtout, it was, in a word, breathtaking. In 1946 the 4½-liter Lago Record made its debut, a striking car utilizing a modified Grand Sport engine and similar styling. Today both these models are prime collectors pieces. There has been a renaissance of interest, especially in the United States, in Lago's luxury cars.

In the late Forties, sadly, compromise, not luxury, was necessary for survival. In 1949, in an attempt to hold onto the sports car market, the Record was scaled down to the Lago Baby, a popular-priced car with a four-cylinder engine developing 120 hp. Later—with an obvious glance at the transatlantic market—the Lago America was introduced, a 2½-liter car available also with a BMW V-8 engine.

Despite such additions to his line, Antony Lago was being spun in an eddy of financial difficulties. Production dropped from around 1,000 cars a year to under 100. In 1951 Lago was forced to give up his works racing team. A group of private owners, headed by Louis Rosier, continued to race his cars, however, taking six wins that year.

In the annals of motor racing, there are a few races that will live as long as men remain attracted to speed. One of these was Le Mans, 1952. Tony Lago never forgot it. Nor did driver Pierre Levegh who had commissioned Lago to build him a car. Between driver and manufacturer the original 4,600 rpm limit of the 4½-liter car had been beefed up to 5,200, and after about 5,000 additional man hours of refining by Levegh and a couple of assistants, the car was ready for Le Mans. Levegh was determined to drive the car himself—for the full twenty-four hours—and win. The full works teams of Jaguar, Aston Martin, Mercedes-Benz and Ferrari opposed him. Nevertheless at the end of twenty-three hours it appeared that Levegh and the Lago car would be the first combination ever to win Le Mans without a driver change. They were ahead and by a wide margin, but the driver behind the wheel had become a robot. Disregarding the pleas of his wife and Lago to turn the car over to his co-driver, failing to recognize even the men in his own crew, Levegh took off—with twenty-five miles between him and the nearest Mercedes and only forty-four minutes to go. Shortly afterward an official car brought an almost lifeless form back to the pits, and a loudspeaker announced the breakdown of Levegh's car. The mechanical failure—a broken connecting rod. The reason—an almost unconscious driver engaging a lower gear than he intended when accelerating away from the corner at Arnage. For years Lago carried the broken bearing bolt in his pocket—a reminder of a glorious moment that might have been.

The odds were, of course, against that moment, and as the years wore on, they mounted against Tony Lago as well. He had remained longer than most of the small and exclusive French motorcar manufacturers, but in the end, he too was enveloped in the complex machinations of the French industrial scene. In 1959 Automobiles Talbot Darracq S.A. was quietly absorbed into the Simca organization. One year later Major Antony Lago was dead.

—*Beverly Rae Kimes*

A two-place competition type tourismo with coachwork by Figoni et Falaschi. Built in 1948, the car had special features including a dual mechanical system throughout, and it is believed to have been raced at Le Mans.

the "A" was for everything

The war that had been called the war to end wars was over. It was the 1920's. The bloom of prosperity that had blossomed soon after the armistice was causing a materialistic boom in many areas of American life. People could afford to buy and use what once were considered luxuries. More people than ever were buying automobiles, for example, and the car most often purchased was the Ford Motor Company's durable Model T.

To aid the war effort, Ford had produced ambulance chassis, Liberty airplane engines, Eagle boats, Fordson tractors, caissons, helmets, two-man tanks and armor plate. Then after a period of crisis in 1920-21, the company finished converting its full facilities back to peacetime manufacture. As the nation's economy began a steep rise, the demand for Model T's more than kept pace with production. Both the Highland Park plant and the relatively new factory near the River Rouge, midway between downtown Detroit and the Henry Ford estate at Fair Lane, were humming busily.

But America's new prosperity proved 'a mixed blessing, for it was accompanied by the public's growing desire for comfort as well as convenience, and refinements as well as utility. The Ford Motor Company was directly affected. In the middle Twenties the Model T was still the best automotive buy, but only for customers who could tolerate its Spartan plainness. By then General Motors was successfully mass-producing the Chevrolet. This was admittedly a costlier car than the T, but since the

latter was sold in a comparatively naked state—lacking even such commonplace niceties as a self-starter and demountable rims—its price could easily rise to within twenty-five per cent of the Chevy's when equipped with what GM considered standard accessories. Moreover, Chevrolets were offered in a variety of colors—in contrast to the post-1913 dictum invariably attributed to Henry Ford that Model T purchasers could have any color they wished so long as it was black. And as part of GM policy, Chevrolet promised an improved model every year. Some years saw only a modest facelifting, but even that could be considered a change of sorts, when compared with Ford's policy of holding fast.

In 1923, despite healthy sales, the signs were all too clear. Ford dealers could see them; so could most executives. The only man who seemed unable, or more likely unwilling, to recognize the storm-clouded horizon was Henry Ford himself. Every day of the business week, Ford and his chief executives met at noon in a pine-paneled corner room of the engineering laboratory at Dearborn, site of the company headquarters. Luncheon was served and eaten, but often it was nearly supper time before the talk at the big round table had subsided.

Outwardly it was a group united in close harmony, but more and more, discordant notes were being heard. The men knew that Ford would brook none of their criticism of the Model T. Thus with charts and statistics

14

Laden with sacks of wheat, a 1928 Model A pickup truck, Ford's perennial workhorse, awaits unloading at the gristmill in Greenfield Village.

they tried to indicate that though production remained high, unsold cars were accumulating in dealers' lots and showrooms. But whenever dealers' complaints were aired at the table, Henry Ford invariably stated, "The Model T is the most perfect automobile in the world," and that was that. For years the men at the round table had nodded in agreement. Now it was apparent to even the most faithful of them that the Model T's state of perfection was only relative, and ephemeral.

Tension increased, as the rebels at the table grew less content to contain their dissatisfaction. They talked among themselves of the need to replace the T's outmoded planetary transmission and to devise something more efficient than Ford's mechanical brakes. They yearned to manufacture an automobile in colors other than black. They were consumed with the idea of making improvements to meet their competition head-on, rather than to cling to accouterments of a past success. Their ally, and their leader by default, was Henry Ford's only son, Edsel. He could have helped them more, perhaps, if he had had less of a fight of his own to attend to.

Henry Ford had been a munificent father, but despite his generosity, it was evident that he had withheld from his son nearly as much as he had given. Edsel had received $1 million in gold on his twenty-first birthday, and at twenty-six he had become president of the Ford Motor Company. He was like a fairy-tale hero, except that in reality, though he bore the

title and wore the crown, he was more pawn than king. His father had not stood down but had merely stepped aside. Henry Ford still held a seat on the board of directors and in effect still owned the company.

Henry and Edsel were opposites, in every possible way. If they had worked together on an equal basis, their constant friction might have sparked productive results. However, they were not equals, and due to circumstance and the nature of their diverse personalities, they rarely clashed in the open. Edsel was a quiet, well-mannered individual who suppressed his feelings to the extent that only his digestive system felt the turmoil of his anger. His father was, conversely, an outspoken and volatile man who never held anything back, least of all anger.

People close to Henry Ford couldn't help being aware of the father's great love and respect for his son. But the fact that Edsel was his antithesis pained him, and he seldom acknowledged it, even to himself. Surely nothing would have pleased Henry Ford more than to have cast a son in his own image. But such was not the case. Edsel Ford was an egalitarian, a man of sensibilities, a businessman with an engineer's regard for design. His father was an autocrat, a ruggedly individualistic product of the Nineteenth Century. The difference between the two can be likened to that between an instrument honed to precision by machine and a tool fashioned from stone by human energy. Both may do the same job well—but differently.

Time was surely overtaking the elder Ford, but he still held the advantage. In addition to a lifetime of some six decades to look back on, Henry Ford had a phenomenal achievement with which to substantiate his peremptory management of the Ford Motor Company. A long time prior, he had made a promise—"I will build a car for the multitudes"—which he had fulfilled in 1908 with the Model T. Within three years the car was being reproduced at a rate of better than three thousand a month and more than forty thousand a year. It was being called the "universal car," and it very nearly was.

Henry Ford had kept his promise to the "multitudes," for he had correctly appraised their needs. He had produced a car that practically anyone could drive, that was inexpensive to maintain and required no special skills to repair. Owning a Model T was a solid guarantee of efficiency and utility on the road, and under any road conditions. Until the third decade of the century, Ford's Tin Lizzie—a nickname bestowed with undoubted affection—fulfilled the needs of the majority of low- and middle-income car buyers, and continued to make converts of those people to whom a motor vehicle still seemed frivolous and unnecessary. Ford's judgment had been sound enough; it was marred only by his failure to realize that consumer needs change with changing times. He assumed illogically that the "multitudes" would always want his stripped-down package in the same dull wrappings.

The Tin Lizzie had been a revolutionary automobile that had helped stir a revolution in auto manufacturing techniques. Because of the number of cars being produced, and the need to produce them swiftly and economically, Henry Ford had become a foremost exploiter of mass production. Through experimentation, he and his engineers had discovered that the moving assembly line, with its several integrated feeders, was the most expeditious means for mass-producing automobiles. The result of this mass production was mass availability: a low price that nearly everyone could afford. In the wake of the Tin Lizzie, roadways began to stretch like slender fingers across the face of the land. Wagon trails became highways, towpaths became thoroughfares, and vast stretches of prairie and pasture yielded access to farms and hamlets, and to other reaches of landscape hitherto remote.

With such a history of achievement to turn to, it is easy to see why Henry Ford thought his judgment indisputable. Since he had been right before, and since nearly half the cars on the road were Fords, there was no reason for him to suppose he was any less right now than he had once been. And though he was a discerning man with a discriminating and canny business sense, he ignored the signs suggesting that his Tin Lizzie's days were numbered. To the exhortations of his executives and entreaties of his dealers, he responded wearily, "Well, gentlemen, so far as I can see, the only trouble with the Ford car is that we can't make it fast enough."

The implication was that the car was not at fault, only the dealers—for failing to sell it fast enough.

Ford had put pressure on his dealers before, and most of them had survived, to the company's eventual profit. In 1921, at the depth of the postwar depression, with foreclosure threatened if Ford failed to repay $75 million in bank loans, Henry Ford achieved what must be considered a financial coup, like it or not. He stepped up production of Model T's and in short order dispensed them throughout his dealer network. Predictably, there were angry outcries, for the cars had been unordered and unwanted. To the protests Ford replied, in effect, "Accept them or forfeit your franchise." And as was customary, the cars were to be paid for in cash upon delivery, with transportation costs billed to the dealers.

Not every franchise holder acquiesced, but few could afford to end their association with a source of product that had earned them a handsome profit and a considerable reputation over the years. The men who lacked capital were forced to borrow the money, and thus in scores of banks around the country, Ford's enormous debt was repaid in part through a series of small loans to individual Ford dealers. That such a coup could be effected was a testament to Henry Ford's acumen. It was also a testimony of the esteem in which the Tin Lizzie was held, for the loans would not have been made at such a time if the car had not been regarded good collateral.

Ford survived the crisis, and the majority of dealers remained loyal. Henry Ford had said repeatedly that nothing was wrong with the Model T that good salesmanship couldn't cure, and he appeared to be right. Granted, he had cut his prices by more than a hundred dollars on some models, but his margin of profit was sustained by a commensurate rise in sales volume. Four years later, as another crisis threatened, he felt he had grounds for insisting that a lack of intensity in the sales effort and not a deficiency in the Model T was the cause of its decline.

He was wrong this time. Some said it was vanity that prevented him from comprehending it. Others said it was his stubbornness or his intractable ego. Perhaps it was neither. What may well have caused him to prolong the life of his Tin Lizzie was his desire to replace it only when he could produce a vehicle as revolutionary as that car had been. The T had taken him four years to develop, and in the years since conception, had become his alter ego. In an interview he once told reporters, "Time spent on your competitors is time lost to your business." The fact that Chevrolet and other low-priced products were beginning to encroach on the T's sales domain was less significant to him than the fact that he had not yet developed a worthy enough successor to the car. He did not want to be

Leslie R. Henry's 1928 Model A phaeton was photographed near the sawmill at Greenfield Village, Dearborn, site of the Henry Ford Museum.

The Greenfield Village post office provides background for the 1931 deluxe roadster (above) owned by Nick Timon. The 1928 standard roadster (below), lacking a rumble seat, was for business rather than sport.

With nickeled cowl lamps and other exterior details, the 1929 town sedan (above) was a Model A aristocrat. In contrast was the functional Tudor, by far the most popular A. The model below is owned by W. H. Leyland.

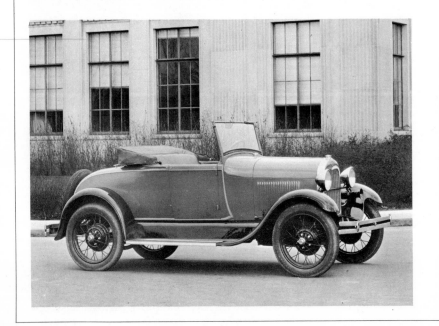

reduced to the status of an imitator. Such was the nature of his pride.

By 1925 the tension at the executive round table was becoming unbearable. Even Henry Ford could feel it. And the obvious fact that his son was among those who opposed him, or at least was critical of him, was a distasteful twisting of his arm. He still refused to abandon the T, but he conceded that the company itself would have to pump new blood into the lagging sales effort.

Breaking a Ford precedent of long standing, he sanctioned the start of a nationwide advertising campaign. Finding that ineffective, he allowed the company to offer the public a $60 package that included rebuilding the engine of any Model T, reupholstering its interior, and repainting its body. This offer was followed by some superficial modifications whose purpose, it seemed, was to assure car buyers that the Ford Motor Company was aware of changing times and was not standing still. The windshield of the Model T was given a somewhat rakish slant; the fenders were cupped; the radiator shell was given a gleaming nickel-plated finish. Further, the car body was lengthened several inches; the chassis was lowered, the radiator raised; the fuel tank was transferred from under the front seat to a position beneath the cowl. And as the ultimate concession to the public's growing style consciousness, the Tin Lizzie stepped out of her basic black shroud and into fawn gray, phoenix brown, gunmetal blue and highland green.

The change was for the better; there was no denying it. But beneath the T's new exterior chugged the same 22½ hp engine on the same well-used chassis. In 1926, Model T production fell by more than a quarter of a million units; sales continued to plummet; unpurchased and possibly unwanted Fords stood row upon row in agencies all over the country. The picture was clear now. Henry Ford could no longer ignore it. On May 25, 1927, newspapers carried the announcement that production of the Model T Ford would be suspended.

The car had typified an era that had passed years before the car itself ceased being made. Or as one Ford executive insisted, "The Model T lasted two years longer than it should have." But though it bowed out in defeat, the car remained a legend, and many people mourned its passing. Numberless farmers, businessmen, housewives and salesmen wrote passionate letters of protest, imploring Ford to continue manufacturing the car. It was reported, too, that an elderly New Jersey lady purchased and stored seven new Model T's so she would not have to change cars for the rest of her life.

There were, in addition, many men who felt that the T should continue to be made and sold alongside its successor. Dealers as a group came to share this view, for once again their loyalty and their mettle were to be tested. When their supply of Model T's was spent, their showrooms would be empty until a new model was produced. And worse, despite only a

trickle of news being issued about the new model, unsold Model T's proved a drug on the market. The dealers who survived the shutdown period depended on the sale of Model T parts and service, and on the faith that Henry Ford would deliver them once more. Ford employees had even less to cling to when assembly lines were halted. At that time, sixty thousand men were laid off in Detroit alone. Their dismissal seemed singularly harsh, coming from a man who had elevated his workers to a five-dollar day, but Henry Ford's mandate had been that a new-car project should not get under way until the last Model T had come out of the shops. Several ideas were under development during the Model T's last year, but little progress was actually made until the spring of 1927. And by then the pressure was on, as dealers and potential car buyers waited, and thousands of men clamored for jobs.

The pace of activity within the Dearborn headquarters was frenzied. Time was money, and everybody knew it; the Ford Motor Company was going to lose more than $100 million during the shutdown period. Henry Ford was inexplicably unperturbed, however. "What in the world do we want of that money?" he said. "Just to keep it in the banks?" His dissatisfaction, in the months to come, was not with the company's financial status, but mainly with his son.

Edsel had his own ideas of what the new Ford car should be, and many of these ideas were in opposition to what his father wanted to do. There were times when antagonism between the two men was so strong that intermediaries had to dart between offices, conveying messages back and forth, striving to keep father and son apart. Not all the messages were actually delivered. Of those that weren't, one directed Edsel to go to California and remain there until summoned back.

Characteristic of cold wars, the conflict between father and son took its toll in time. As Edsel and Henry Ford wrangled over such points as brakes and transmission, the production date of the new car seemed farther and farther away. There were other delays, too, caused by many niggling problems that had to be solved. One of these is recalled by Leslie R. Henry in his book *Henry's Fabulous Model A*. Mr. Ford, it seems, was insistent that the new car have a cowl-mounted gravity fuel tank. Since a number of states had questioned the safety of such an arrangement, design of the new car was suspended for a time until state officials could be persuaded that no real hazard was involved. Says Mr. Henry, "Actual tests demonstrated that the Ford fuel tank would not explode even if the gasoline caught fire when filling the tank."

Although the months passed and funds continued to drain away, there was no waning of interest on the public's part. Rumors appearing almost daily in the press kept the public consciousness aglow and fanned enthusiasm. Despite the lack of official information about the new car, anticipation ran so high that half a million persons ultimately paid deposits on the car before they had seen it or found out its price. And everybody waited.

The new car's birth was slow in coming. Every problem solved by engineers seemed only to lead to other problems still to be solved. One thing was clear: neither Henry nor Edsel Ford was going to be completely satisfied by the final package. Compromises had been necessary and unavoidable. It was hoped, however, that they would not compromise the product and that the new car would represent the best aspects of two distinct schools of thought, the best ideas of two totally different but unquestionably creative men.

By midsummer 1927 the costly retooling process was in full swing, and unemployed craftsmen were eagerly returning to their jobs. Nearly all 5,580 parts of the new Ford were new, so factory layouts had to be changed, and the mechanism of all Ford plants had to be completely reconstructed. Some fifteen thousand machine tools had to be replaced; another twenty-five thousand had to be rebuilt. Five million dollars' worth of dies and fixtures had to be redesigned and rearranged. The operation that was taking place was the costliest and most elaborate that had yet been attempted. And while the parts were being made and the millwrights, die and pattern makers were at work, the final design of the car was still being determined. With so much invested and so much at stake, no detail was too small to escape close scrutiny.

Outside Ford plants, and inside too, suspense continued to mount. With no official word from Ford either to confirm or deny the rumors, every "leak" and murmur received attention; all contained fragments of plausibility, and any one of them might have been true. Stories varied from boasts that the new Ford would be radically different, and cheaper than the T, to reports that the car would be "purely defensive" and would cost much more than the T.

It was reported, for example, that the car was to be a cross between a Ford and a Lincoln and thus would be called a Linford. It was also reported that the car would be named after one of Henry Ford's oldest and dearest friends, Thomas Edison. The first story earned more acceptance than the second after a newspaper published the "fact" that a nameplate manufacturer in Columbus, Ohio, was engaged in turning out Linford emblems.

Rumors to the contrary, nobody knew what the new car was called, or how it would look, until shortly before its debut. However, many people claimed they had seen the car and that it resembled a small Marmon or a diminutive version of the Lincoln or LaSalle. The Ford company did nothing to contradict this speculation, but continued to carry out its successful secrecy campaign. When dealers' shipments reached their destinations, crowds of people waited at railroad stations and on street corners, hoping to glimpse the mystery Ford. But the cars were transported from freight cars to showrooms under canvas shrouds—not even a hubcap could

be seen. The suspense was such that *The New York Times* was moved to report, "The tension has been strained to the breaking point."

On November 28, 1927, the first of a five-day series of ads consumed full pages of two thousand daily newspapers around the country. Still, the tension mounted. Not till the fifth day was the public told what the car looked like and how much it would cost. The cloak of secrecy extended into newspaper offices too. Matrixes for the final day's ad were shipped in bundles sealed with a printed warning that they were not to be opened until press time. Prices were wired to individual papers only in time to make the morning editions, not before. Ford was taking no chances on having a last-minute leak mar a campaign that purportedly had cost more than a million dollars and assuredly was worth several times more.

At its first public showing in New York, in January, 1928, the police were called out to hold back the mobs surging into Madison Square Garden. Fifty thousand New Yorkers made orders and paid cash deposits on the new car. In St. Paul, Minnesota, twenty-five thousand persons turned out, despite sub-zero temperatures. In Cleveland, mounted police had to be summoned to protect Ford show windows. Elsewhere—in Denver, Berlin, Madrid, London—the enthusiasm was the same. In the U.S. alone, according to estimates, ten million persons inspected the new car in its first thirty-six hours on display.

The new car was neither a Linford nor an Edison, and it was not an imitator. The car, called the Model A, was named after the Ford Motor Company's first passenger car, which had been built in 1903. The A was certainly a departure from the Model T, but though it was slightly more costly than its predecessor, it sold for less than the competing Chevrolet. The two-door, or in Ford lexicon the Tudor, sedan was priced at $495, which was the exact price of the Model T and $100 cheaper than a comparable Chevy. The four-door, or Fordor, sedan sold for $570, only $30 more than the T and $125 less than the Chevrolet.

The new car may have been close in price to the Model T, but all the two cars really had in common, besides the Ford emblem, were transverse springs. A standard, three-speed shift had replaced the T's planetary transmission. Instead of rear-wheel brakes, there were four-wheel mechanical brakes. The flywheel magneto had given way to a coil-and-battery ignition. There were instruments on the dashboard and lights by which to read them. There was a foot accelerator for the first time, a logical addition, for gears were no longer shifted by foot pedals. There was laminated safety glass in the windshield, a feature that Ford was first in the low-priced field to incorporate. Other features included hydraulic shock

---

This handsome 1929 coupé, with patent-leather sheen, was Henry Ford's personal car. It is shown by the old workshop in Greenfield Village.

The convertible sedan, one of the last Model A's, appears above and on page 14. Below is a fire engine built on an AA chassis, owned by P. E. Ondo and photographed at the Ft. Meyers Laboratory, Greenfield Village.

The replica in Greenfield Village of Luther Burbank's birthplace is the background for Harold Anderson's 1929 special coupé (above). The 1928 business coupé (below) was a two-passenger car with a large trunk space.

absorbers, motor-operated windshield wipers, a unique oiling process effected by combining pump, splash and gravity feed, and a cooling system facilitated by a centrifugal water pump. Each model was available in Niagara blue, gunmetal blue, Arabian sand and two shades of Dawn gray—except the Fordor sedan, which came in a quartet of more exclusive colors.

The Model A engine was a four-cylinder affair with a bore of $3\frac{7}{8}$ inches and a stroke of $4\frac{1}{4}$ inches. It developed 40 hp at 2,200 rpm, nearly twice the power of the Model T, and its top speed was 65 mph.

The most significant aspect of the new Ford, at least so far as the manufacturer was concerned, was its sliding-gear transmission. Henry Ford had been solidly against it in the early stages of the car's development. He called the shifting gear a "crunch gear" and insisted that it would never withstand the abrasion of constant use. Privately he felt that by including the sliding-gear apparatus, his company would be imitating others. He wanted his nineteen-year-old "three on the floor" transmission to be retained in the new model.

For a while he pondered the idea of developing an automatic transmission for the Model A, but his associates finally convinced him that the odds against producing such a device were unfavorable, and that even if it proved feasible, many years' development would probably be needed. So he conceded. Actually, he was anticipating by some ten years the development of Hydramatic, which is a planetary type transmission with an automatic clutch activated by hydraulic pressure. Many people believed that Henry Ford's business methods were dated and singularly arbitrary, but it must be said that in terms of mechanical and engineering innovation —perhaps not in styling—he strived always to be ahead of his time. The Model A, produced in a spirit of compromise, must have been a little disappointing to him.

Even Edsel Ford admitted, "There is nothing radical about the new car." More important, of course, was the fact that it *was* a new car. The car-buying public, and Ford dealers as well, were more excited by the car's arrival—at long last—than by any single facet of its design. Generally the A contained most of the refinements the public had been clamoring for, and it was priced right for mass sales. There was only one difficulty. Ford was unable to produce enough cars, at the outset, when the clamor was at its peak, to satisfy the demand. Sidney Strong, who at one time had the oldest Ford dealership in Minnesota and is now executive director of the Early American Museum in Silver Springs, Florida, recalls, "Even a month after announcement date, most Ford assembly plants had a mere handful of Model A's, and throughout January, 1928, disparaging rumors were rife. To prove the car's existence, representatives were dispatched from branch plants to drive from town to town throughout the land and spend a few hours at each Ford dealership, demonstrating the car." Until then, most customers had seen the car only in photographs.

With so much pressure from the public, and urgent pleas from dealers, it is reasonable to assume the Ford Motor Company would become defensive. Not at all. Henry Ford's rigidity toward his dealers was unalterable. Mr. Strong recalls being summoned, along with other local dealers, to the office of one of Ford's regional managers. There the group was informed that they were still just Model T dealers and that each of them had to prove that he was qualified to become a seller of Model A's. According to Mr. Strong, before any new cars could be delivered, the dealers were directed to show evidence that they had accomplished the following:

"Shops and showrooms were to be placed in order as 'A Models' of cleanliness. Neat new parts bins, freshly labeled, had to be readied to receive new parts. Shops had to be provided with new equipment and mechanics trained to properly service this completely new Ford, to maintain it as the 'engineering marvel' it was. Another requirement was to prove the ability of a dealership to operate without dependence on the profits from new-car sales. The regional manager gave his assurance that accomplishment of these requirements would be rewarded with perhaps 'two, three, five or even ten more Model A's,' as each dealer qualified. . . ."

The lagging supply of cars, plus Ford's reduction of commissions soon after the depression began, forced many dealers to make a difficult decision: either go out of business or take the risk of bankruptcy. Some of them dropped their Ford franchise and began selling other cars. The Model A was not in a class by itself, after all. It presented a challenge its competitors quickly managed to meet. Within a year, the Chrysler Corporation brought out its Plymouth, which featured hydraulic brakes and much-publicized "floating power." In 1929, Chevrolet introduced a six-cylinder engine and geared a potent sales campaign to the notion that six cylinders could now be had for the price of four. The minute changes made in the Model A were insufficient to stem the tide against it. In 1932 the car was dropped, and Henry Ford made news once again when he unveiled his low-priced V-8.

During a four-year life span, nearly five million Model A's were produced. But long before that total was reached, the car's obsolescence was evident. The pace of progress had increased immeasurably since the heyday of the Model T. From his Model A experience, Henry Ford realized there was a need to modify some of his marketing notions and to engage in active, annual competition with other makers. Thus the car was significant beyond its engineering assets and the celebrity of its late arrival. It passed quietly from the scene in the spring of 1932, but with its demise came a new and inexplicable wave of respect and affection for the car it had been. Today there are enough Model A's licensed and in good running order, in the U.S. alone, to guarantee it against extinction. And Model A owners are a devoted lot; if they have anything to do with it, the car will never, ever be forgotten.

—*Mervyn Kaufman*

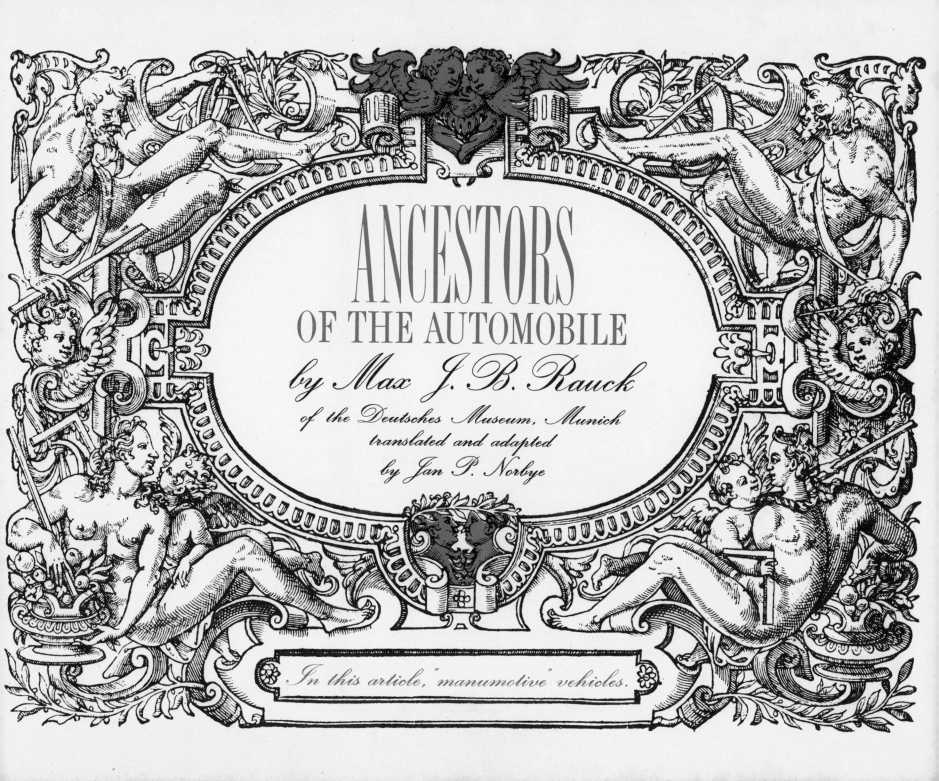

ANCESTORS
OF THE AUTOMOBILE

by Max J. B. Rauck

of the Deutsches Museum, Munich

translated and adapted

by Jan P. Norbye

In this article, "manumotive" vehicles.

From the time man's reasoning powers were developed, he has stretched the limits of his perception in an effort to penetrate the vast unknown. Largely through mysticism, aided now and then by forays into the occult, he has tried to see beyond an immediate future made predictable by regularly recurring events.

Visions and prophecies are as fascinating to men today as to their forbears. At the last engineering congress of the SAE, men in responsible positions with some of the world's largest industrial enterprises devoted half a day to some airy conjecturing on how the automobiles of the Twenty-First Century might seem. Each participant had definite ideas about the car of the future and its mechanical make-up, but no one offered even a broad plan for achieving construction of vehicles propelled and controlled by devices that are still beyond the extent of technological knowledge.

Current prophecies are not much better supported scientifically than those of Roger Bacon, a learned English monk of the Thirteenth Century, and other visionaries of antiquity. Ancient Egyptian, Chinese, Greek and Roman artists depicted horseless chariots and other self-propelled vehicles, but the motive power of each of these contrivances was never specified, and at the time viewers may have assumed it was of divine origin. Roger Bacon offered no clues toward solving the mystery when he wrote, "With the aid of science and art alone, it is possible to make wagons roll in a fixed direction without the help of draught animals . . ." It has been established, however, that man's early dreams of a carriage with the ability to propel itself led to a search for motive power in all known areas of nature.

Stephan Farffler, a cripple, built himself a hand-powered carriage for traveling to church.

Constructing the carriage itself was no problem. Approximately six thousand years ago, not long after a Mesopotamian potter devised a crude wheel to aid him in his craft, vehicles of both two and four wheels were being built. They were dependent, for motive power, on donkeys and horses, and were so cumbersome that they could not be driven for long at speed.

Man has always been obsessed with speed and has never relinquished his dream of traveling swifter than the wind. Though the scientists and inventors of antiquity could not build self-propelled vehicles, there was nothing to stop the artists and visionaries from drawing them. Sailboats existed long before the wheel, so it was inevitable that sail-cars should also be built. And the search for other and more controllable power sources went on, but man could still only utilize the most primitive ones.

The Egyptians and the Chinese began to experiment with wind-powered carriages almost four thousand years ago. Alexander the Great used gravity to propel the wagons of his invading troops as they swept down the mountain slopes of Asia Minor. Hero of Alexandria knew of steam power and used it for opening the doors of religious temples, but neither he nor any other Egyptian ever built a steam car. The passing of millenia brought the refinement of wheeled vehicles, but opened up no new sources of power. By medieval times man had come to rely mainly on his own muscle for the controlled propulsion of lightweight wheeled vehicles.

The idea of muscle-powered vehicles dates back to the days of Babylon and Pharaonic Egypt. Later, both Greeks and Romans built man-propelled cars, mainly for military purposes and religious processions, and these ma-

Elie Richard's manumotive car, built in 1690, required the aid of a servant in back—to pedal.

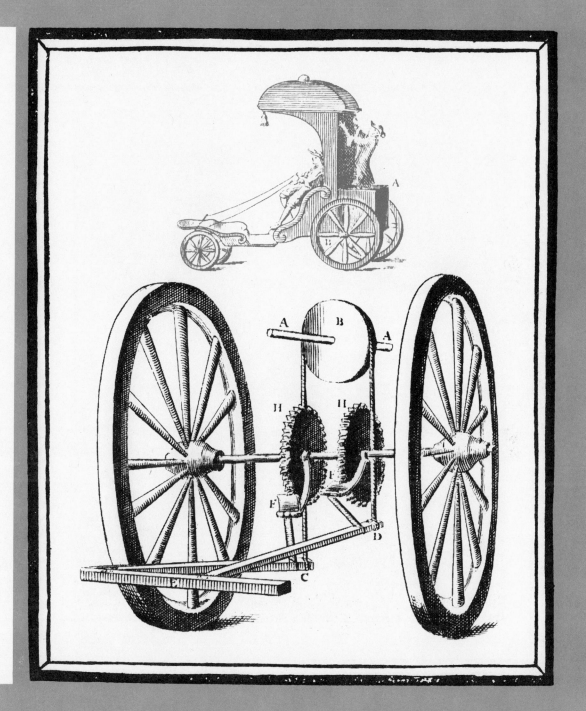

chines remained tools of office and of transport for warriors and high priests. Wheeled vehicles were not yet used for moving goods or groups of personnel from place to place. Although the Romans were great roadbuilders, they did not materially aid development of the man-propelled car. And the collapse of the Roman Empire created a lapse of more than a thousand years in the construction of such vehicles.

With new manifestations of man's desire for self-propulsion, the vehicles that were then built had the benefit of new discoveries in metallurgy, chemistry and physics. And workable ideas on transmission and gearing, many of which were first propounded by Leonardo da Vinci, found practical application in the "manumotive" vehicles of the Seventeenth and Eighteenth Centuries. These contrivances were conceived by inventors and visionaries throughout the world.

A mechanic in Nuremberg, Johann Hautzsch (1595-1670), who was well known for his construction of fire-fighting apparatus, built two man-propelled "triumphal" cars. The first one, which is pictured on page 24, was completed in 1649. It was adorned with a dragon's head at the front to further the illusion that the vehicle was gas-propelled, since smoke would issue from its mouth at the driver's command. In reality there were four men hidden inside, working hand cranks to make the wheels turn. The Swedish Crown Prince, Karl Gustaf, bought the car for 500 Reichsmark when he visited Nuremberg. When he took the throne in 1654 as King Karl, the triumphal wagon took part in the coronation parade in Stockholm.

King Frederick III of Denmark was so impressed with the car that he could not rest until Hautzsch had built him a similar one. It was

In the two-man Maillard car the driver turned a crank connected by spur gears to the wheels.

completed in 1663, and was of an improved design with slightly higher speed than the first one, although neither could ever maintain walking pace on level ground.

In Altdorf, Switzerland, a partly paralyzed watchmaker named Stephan Farffler built two small invalid carriages, one in 1685 and one in 1688. He made the first one mainly to take himself to church on Sundays. It was a three-wheeler with a hand crank attached to the front wheel—for steering as well as propelling the vehicle. The second carriage was improved in detail design and was also used by the watchmaker. It was preserved until 1944 when it was destroyed during an air raid. Farffler's cars were mechanically inefficient, and friction losses were so high that travel over long distances was out of the question. But these vehicles received much attention at the time and may have inspired a whole generation of man-powered vehicles.

About the end of the Seventeenth Century the hand crank began to disappear, and pedal wagons came into vogue. One exception is the Maillard vehicle of 1731, which utilized a hand crank coupled to a train of spur gears transmitting power to the driving wheels.

Doctor Elie Richard, who came from the Isle of Ré, across the bay from La Rochelle in western France, built and used the first pedal wagon to be in regular operation for a sustained period of time. When he lived and worked in Paris, Dr. Richard used this car for his business calls all over town.

A report on this vehicle was given by Jacques Ozanam, a well-known member of the Royal Academy of Science in Paris, and published in 1696 in *Récréations Mathématiques et Physiques*. The report even showed pictures of the

A smaller Maillard carriage, planned in 1731, had room for only a driver, who did all the work.

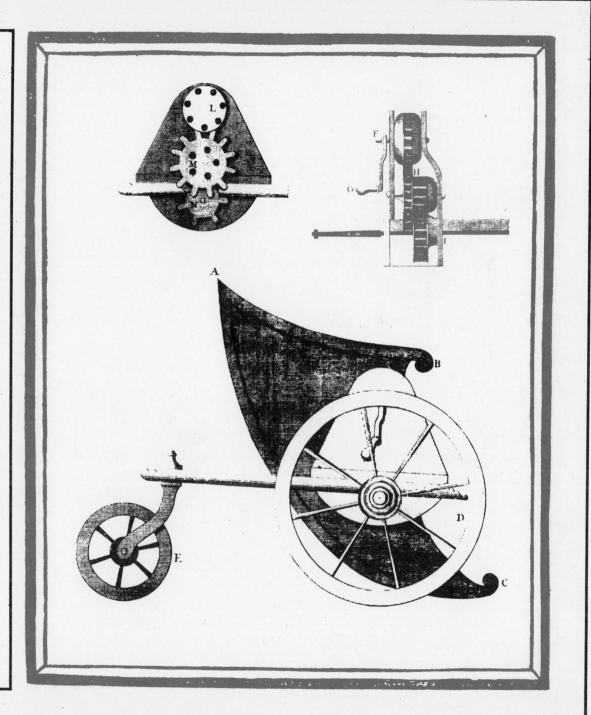

pedal wagon. Dr. Richard steered it from the front seat, and his servant stood behind, working two pedals in alternating motion. The power was transmitted by means of a rope around a roller coupled to a gear train connected to the rear wheels. The same basic design was copied by many pedal-car builders in several countries.

The first traffic accident occurred because no brakes were fitted on Dr. Richard's car, and it ended its last drive by ramming into a wall. But he had shown that such conveyances were possible, and at the beginning of the Eighteenth Century, pedal cars were common in the big cities of France and England, and imitations were being made in Germany and in the northern Italian cities of Genoa, Padua and Bologna. For the rich man, a pedal car enabled him to take a lazy promenade in his garden at the expense of his servant's muscular energy.

The French historian John Grand-Carteret quoted contemporary opinion on these vehicles in his book *La Voiture de Demain:* "Vehicles with hidden mechanisms travel around and look like an invention of the devil. Yet it is a wonderful thing to see people being transported in this fashion."

In spite of the fact that pedal cars became well known, there were still many inventors who preferred cranks and levers. Then in the Eighteenth Century came mechanical wheelchairs. On many of these the transmission was so simplified that they could be hand-driven by turning the actual road wheels. In April, 1748, the famous mechanic Jacques de Vaucanson presented his self-driven wagon before King Louis XV. It had a transmission system consisting of gears and chains, and the King was given a demonstration of the car in the palace square. He was

The Baynes carriage was to be propelled by a lever, imitating the movements of a man walking.

so enthralled that he immediately ordered a car, and he told Vaucanson that "ordinary people will think you are a wizard."

Similar cars obtained widespread notoriety in other places. A professor at Trinity College in Dublin delivered a speech about the problems of self-propelled vehicles to his students in 1766. Three years later a teacher, John Vevers, at Reigate School in Surrey wrote about pedal cars for London magazines. He wisely concluded that "speed was, above all, dependent upon the activity of the pedaler." Two anonymous citizens of the Alsatian town of Strasbourg built a carriage that has been ascertained to have been pedal driven. This vehicle seems to have been the first to use a steering wheel. An authentic report stated that there was a small wheel to control direction—situated in the center of the car, at its forward end.

There came a point in the development of the automobile's ancestors wherein the man-propelled vehicle reached a bifurcation, just as in the history of man, a number of races sprang from the evolution of the species Homo sapiens.

After the arrival and commercial exploitation of Newcomen and Watt's steam engines, it became apparent to most men who took an interest in mechanized transport that the future of motive power for horseless carriages lay in the direction of harnessing fuel to yield the maximum thermal energy, and not in the primitive practice of fixing a lackey to a treadmill.

Richard Trevithick constructed his first road locomotive in 1801, and in 1815 George Stephenson laid the cornerstone of the entire railroad industry by taking out a patent for coupling the connecting rods of the steam engine directly to the wheels of the locomotive. But the beginnings

Snowden's idea of a horse-powered house was majestic, but not practicable for man or beast.

Moving this English-built vehicle required maximum energy and produced maximum discomfort.

of a network of railroad and steam-coach lines in England did not deter some inventors from fixing their attention on self-moving vehicles propelled solely by human muscle. The work of these men is a matter of only semi-relevance to the automotive historian, but it is fascinating in the richness of its variety.

One such man was Freiherr Carl von Drais, who in December, 1813, presented a man-propelled car before the Czar of Russia, when the latter visited Mannheim. The Czar liked the vehicle so well that he gave the constructor a diamond ring as a prize for the invention. After that, von Drais went to the Congress of Vienna to be honored as an inventor. A contemporary report shows that the blasé Viennese had not lost their perspective. These words were published in a local paper on October 30, 1814: "Suddenly a beautiful four-wheeled carriage without horses came out of the gate and drove at extraordinary speed across the Bergplatz and the Michaelsplatz. Two persons sat in it and steered. It has been invented by a visiting mechanic who hopes to sell it in Vienna."

The road surfaces then presented a considerable hazard to four-wheeled vehicles, so von Drais turned to two- and three-wheelers. In 1817 he became the inventor of the so-called running wheel, or "Draisine," as it was later called, which had two wheels in line and was propelled by the rider's legs pushing against the ground. With this "hobby horse" on wheels, von Drais began the history of the bicycle. And in 1819 he built a three-wheeled "Draisine" with steering on the front wheels.

Other builders of remarkable self-propelled vehicles were Deacon Roth and Chaplain Superior Kittlinger in Schwabach in 1816. From an eyewitness account, it is known that their vehicle, which was enormous, ran on April 15, 1818. It was a four-wheeled carriage with four pushrods working as mechanical feet, all stemming against the ground at the same time to push the carriage forward. In two hours this vehicle could cover the distance a man would normally walk in an hour and a quarter. Ten people were needed to drive and steer. Spectators noted that the stilts moved slowly and often lost their grip on the road surface.

Strangely enough, in view of the understanding of gear transmissions that most builders of mechanical cars had displayed, some steam-carriage pioneers were inclined to favor mechanical feet over axle transmissions. One such inventor was William Brunton in 1813, and later examples include David Gordon and James Boydell in 1837. Even as late as 1892, Emil Kiebitz of Rossla took out a patent for a leg-type propulsion system.

It is on record that in 1818 Anton Heller requested financial aid from the Royal Academy of Science, Munich, for the construction of a man-propelled vehicle. He built a model with mechanical feet activated in alternating motion by clockwork springs. An expert from the Academy declared that all such vehicles were nonsense and useless toys, because man could always move faster, easier and better on foot.

Also in 1818, the journal of the Arts and Crafts in Bavaria reported that a mechanic named Meyer, of Hallstadt, had a Drais car that he often drove in the city. Meyer also made a three-wheeled pedal car with drive on the single rear wheel. In an utterly sanguine mood, he later built a car that would carry four persons, with only a single man to propel it, by

A velocipede patented in 1869 was designed for its driver to steer and pedal at the same time.

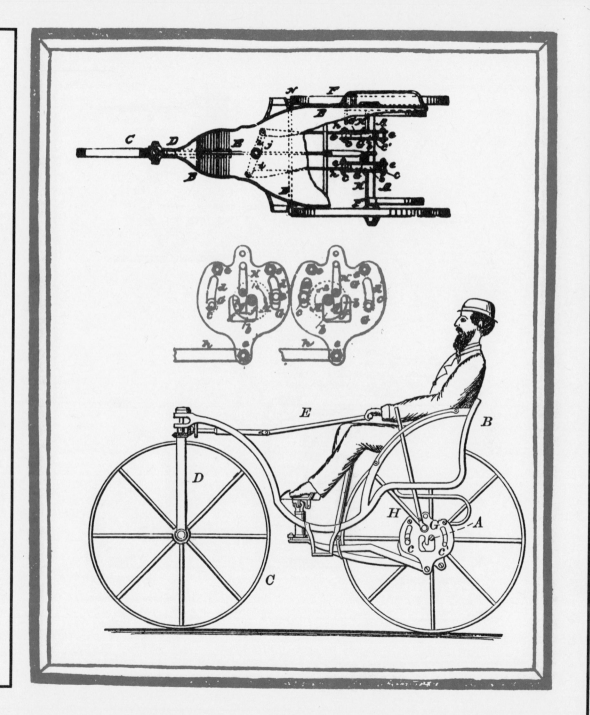

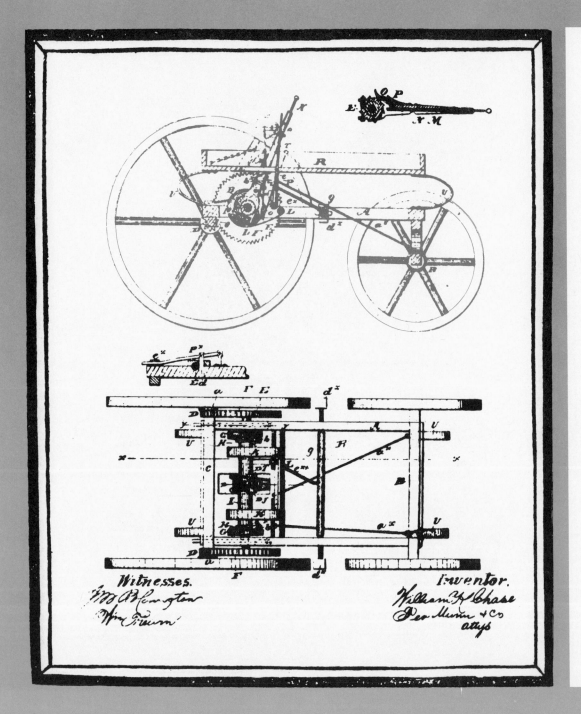

Witnesses.
M B Lewiston
Wm Brown

Inventor.
William H. Chase
Geo Munn + Co
attys

working the pedals in the back of the chassis.

One vehicle of this era has been preserved and can be seen in the Turin automotive museum. The machine was built by Gaetano Brianza of Milan in 1819 and was hand-driven by means of levers connected via cranks to the rear axle. The carriage had a horse's head of papier-mâché attached to its front end and was presumably used in carnival processions. The single front wheel did the steering. This remarkable vehicle was also used for racing, and there are records of a race being held on May 5, 1819, in Milan.

In 1824 a patent was issued to the English mechanic William Francis Snowden for a self-propelled vehicle driven by horses. The animals were carried along on a treadmill working the rear axle via gears, and contemporary drawings indicate that this was supposed to be a two-story vehicle. The horses were on the lower floor, hidden inside; a passenger compartment was on top. There is no evidence that the carriage was ever built, however.

Another attempt to employ animal power was patented in 1817 by a Buffalo, New York, inventor. The chassis drawing shows a three-wheeler with steering on the single rear wheel. The front wheels supported a wide treadmill with at least two dogs inside it. A French patent for a similar carriage was granted to Narcisse Huret as late as 1875.

But it appears that the mainstream of inventors devoted to mechanical vehicles preferred manpower and concentrated on improving transmission systems. About 1825, the Frenchman Salomon Fehr suggested a contraption that had hand levers connected to a crankshaft. And in 1829 a patent was issued to Pierre Auguste

A clockwork-spring-driven vehicle was patented by an American inventor, W. H. Chase, in 1866.

Caron and his partner Armengaud for a three-wheeler known as Colibri or Fugitive. The transmission comprised two pedals with a spring-loaded balancing system.

None of the inventors was disturbed by the fact that his vehicle was a fairly complicated gadget. The most courageous ones in this respect may have been Parker and Bramley of England, who built a car with two-man drive in 1830. The front driver not only steered; he worked a hand crank and a set of pedals. The passenger was only slightly less busy; he lay on his stomach working his own hand cranks and pedals, which were all connected to the same axle. Obviously it was not a particularly pleasurable way to travel.

A pedal car patent was taken out in 1830 by Eloi Xavier Jullien, and in 1839 Revis of Cambridge built an improved type of machine with a three-wheeled chassis and a hand-cranked transmission based on the ideas of Richard Merriweather. There is a contemporary sketch of a similar wagon built by Dr. Ernst Alban (1791-1856), a German pioneer of high-pressure steam engines, and Franz Kurtz of Jülich near Aix-la-Chapelle built a pedal car in 1840.

Then there was a number of optimistic inventors who thought a car could be driven by a huge clockwork spring. A drawing of such a car, made in 1846 by mechanic Franz Gustav Wolf, is preserved in the City Museum of Ellbogen in Bohemia. The spring could be wound in five minutes and was supposed to propel the vehicle for a somewhat longer period. The patent literature of almost every country makes reference to all types of spring-propelled mechanical vehicles. For instance, between 1866 and 1897, forty-five American patents were

Pedaling this bicycle-carriage was not supposed to jar the aplomb of even the most delicate lady.

issued for this type of propulsion. The overwhelming majority of these patent ideas were never fulfilled, and of those that were, none ran successfully.

The Science Museum in South Kensington, London, contains a four-wheeled man-powered wagon built by an English coachmaker, J. Ward, in 1850 or 1851, as well as a lightweight three-wheeler of unknown origin. Both have been restored. They are driven by pedals activated by the driver himself. A number of four-wheeled vehicles existed in Britain at the time, and they were known as "homomotive" carriages. At the Crystal Palace Exhibition in 1851, self-driven cars were shown by three constructors. The most successful were those built by Willard Sawyer of Dover, who was active in the business during the years 1850 to 1864. They were mostly four-wheelers but differed individually in their specifications. One of Sawyer's vehicles even had brakes. Sawyer also built pedal wagons for children, and larger models with up to six seats called "Sociables." In 1851 he drove himself from Dover to London, and in 1858 he delivered a pedal car to the Prince of Wales.

The vehicles built by Andrews of Dublin also became well known. One of his Dublin three-wheelers from 1876 is now in the Science Museum. A two-seat three-wheeler built by Jules Boison in 1860 has been preserved in the Automobile Museum at Compiègne, France. In the late Nineteenth Century, there were many muscle-powered vehicles built for children, often disguised to look like horses. The rocking motions of the mechanical horse were transferred via cranks to the driving wheels.

A projected road "Draisine" patented in 1868 by Adolf Beyhl never progressed beyond the

This early "bicycle," with rococco seat, was driven by levers instead of chain and sprocket.

drawing board stage, and his patent privilege was withdrawn because he failed to build the machine. On the other hand, a south German postman named Zink used a three-wheeled carriage of his own construction on his official rounds at Wolfertshausen in the vicinity of Memmingen. The carriage was propelled by hand levers and cranks, and the driver steered the front wheel with his feet. It was clearly no pleasure vehicle, but designed for transport duty. It can be inspected today in the Museum of Two-Wheel Vehicles in Neckarsulm, Germany.

The years 1863 to 1865, after Lenoir had driven his gas-engined car from Paris to Joinville-le-Pont and back without mishap, saw the manufacture of a bicycle that had a pedal-and-crank transmission on the front wheel begin in the Michaux factories. Some time later, pedal cranks became common also on three- and four-wheelers.

Experiments with passenger quadricycles began in Berlin in 1889 with a four-wheeled velocipede built by Dumstrey and Junck. It was reputedly delivered to China for ricksha service. About the same time, a state vehicle with bicycle-type transmission, built by the Laurie & Marner Company of London, was delivered to the Emir of Afghanistan.

Now and then, some inventors would propose construction of special vehicles to run on ice and snow. The Coventry Machinist Company delivered a curious five-wheel man-powered car, possibly for use on the desert sands, to the Sultan of Morocco about 1890. Two wheels drove, two wheels trailed, and one wheel steered. Four men were needed to propel it.

The last of the optimists who devoted their time to large tricycles and quadricycles was

Ganswindt, the most persistent muscle power adherent, tried to compete with horse-drawn taxis.

Hermann Ganswindt of Schöneberg near Berlin. He conceived the idea of starting a commercial taxi service with man-propelled three-wheelers, thinking it would be lucrative. He was not afraid of competition from motor vehicles, because he was certain they would not have a power and speed advantage over his cycle-taxi in city traffic. The first experiment with a Ganswindt taxi took place in Berlin in 1894, and several newspapers commented favorably on it. One paper said: "The new horseless vehicle attracted great attention on its travels around the Magdeburger Platz and in the Lützowstrasse. It is as new as it is extraordinary. You sit in the middle of the carriage which travels speedily through the streets, and in the back stands the driver who steers and works the pedals with his feet. As quickly as this machine will run, it can also be brought to a stop by pressure on the brake."

Two of the Ganswindt vehicles were exhibited at the Munich Sports Fair. The carriage weighed 165 pounds and was intended for three persons including the driver. To negotiate hills better, the gear ratio could be altered by moving the pivot point on the treadles.

The Berlin Fire Department began to take an interest in muscle-powered vehicles in 1893. The department turned to several well-known bicycle manufacturers about the production of such machines, but no company was interested. What was required, specifically, was a machine that would carry six men and their equipment. Since Ganswindt was the man who built a pedal carriage with sufficient freight capacity, he demonstrated it to the Berlin Fire Department in 1894. The demonstration was successful, as far as speed was concerned. The vehicle actually

This two-passenger ricksha-like velocipede underwent shakedown excursions in Berlin in 1889.

traveled faster than the horse-drawn fire engines, but the firemen in charge of pedaling were soon exhausted and arrived at the scene of the fire out of breath. The attempt by Ganswindt and the Berlin Fire Department to replace horse-drawn vehicles was a failure. Yet only six years later, motor vehicles driven by steam or electricity took over from the horses.

About the turn of the Twentieth Century, small four-wheeled carriages, mainly fitted with rubber tires, were built both in Europe and in America. They were generally steered by the driver's feet, while his arms worked the propelling levers. This motion was converted to rotary motion via cranks on the axle. Such cars remained popular for decades but were eventually replaced by bicycles and tricycles. To this day, singular experiments with man-propelled vehicles are made, and patents are applied for and even issued. Inventors continually toy with such ideas as flywheel drive with supplementary spring devices, just as there are still some souls who waste time and money on the invention of a *perpetuum mobile*.

As recently as 1935, a mechanical car known as the Velocar was exhibited in the Paris auto show. It had pedals, a crank-and-chain transmission just like a bicycle but was fitted with seats just like a car. This type of quadricycle enjoyed a brief revival during World War II, especially in Italy. In fact, three- and four-wheeled carriages with various forms of man-powered drive appear in all times of distress and attendant fuel shortages, despite the fact that history has shown repeatedly that the innate power in one man's body is insufficient to drive vehicles with more than two wheels over long distances. ✥

A three-wheeler with pedals and chain drive was assembled for the Emir of Afghanistan in 1890.

THE FLAWS IN THE NEW FORMULA ONE

by Paul Frère

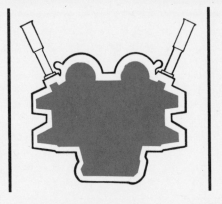

Although some time has passed since the Fédération Internationale de l'Automobile (FIA) announced major revisions of its Formula One racing specifications, the air of controversy that announcement precipitated shows no sign of clearing. Coventry Climax plans to suspend its production of racing engines before the new formula goes into effect next January. And Colin Chapman has hinted darkly that with Coventry Climax out of the picture, he foresees no future participation of his Lotus racing cars in Formula One events.

A more conciliatory, albeit antithetical, voice was raised last March by a group of British car builders who petitioned the FIA's Commission Sportive Internationale to raise the engine displacement limits of the new formula. Obviously these carmakers were hopeful of using existing American V-8 and Ferrari V-12 engines in their new Formula One Grand Prix cars. The reason: building new engines that would not only comply with the formula but would also be capable of winning races will involve a great deal of time, experimentation and money.

As of January 1st, reciprocating and rotary piston engines of either 1½ liters supercharged or 3 liters unblown will receive equal standing. Turbines will be permitted, with no limitation except that they comply with the minimum

weight specifications of 1,100 pounds set for piston cars. In addition, all piston engines will have to operate on 100-octane fuel.

Obviously, there *will* be cars built to suit the Grand Prix formula, despite the present controversy. But building engines for these cars will be costly and complicated, whether manufacturers choose a highly developed 3-liter engine (with at least twelve cylinders to start with, and more eventually) or a multi-stage-supercharged 1500 cc. Even the comparatively simple Wankel type engine, which also qualifies under the formula, would be complicated, if made competitive, and its developmental costs would be greater than those of other configurations.

Turbine engines may be an unwelcome surprise at next year's Formula One events. High-performance gas turbines can be built easily, and with no FIA limitation placed on fuel consumption, it would not be necessary to provide them with heat exchangers. Further, turbines would provide high outputs of power without adding to engine size or weight. Under the rules proposed, throttle response would cease being a problem, for the compression turbine could be kept at its optimum speed, and the exhaust flow it produces would simply be expelled into the atmosphere during the short spells when power is not needed (i.e., when the brakes are being

applied, which is the only time a racing car does not require power). Even if gas turbines gained wide acceptance, little benefit would be gained from racing with them; the development of the turbine for passenger car use seems to have no practical utility at this point.

All things considered, I believe the revised formula is fundamentally wrong. First of all, there is no technical or practical reason why a supercharged 1½-liter engine should be equated with a 3-liter unblown unit. Certainly no power relationship exists between these two types of engines. In fact, the new formula is really no more than a basis for a disguised form of handicap racing in which 1½-liter engines are granted superchargers to offset smaller displacement.

With a 1,100-pound minimum weight imposed on the unfinished car, the formula does not allow much scope for the ingenuity of manufacturers to gain greater speed by reducing the weight and bulk of their cars, instead of increasing power output. Speed thus will have to be gained the costly way—by raising the number of cylinders in order to achieve higher rotational speeds and higher specific output.

Under the new formula, the lessons learned in the pre-1952 era, during which 1½-liter supercharged engines were pitted against 4½-liter atmospheric engines, are useless. Why? Because the use of 100-octane fuel will be mandatory. In the highly supercharged engines of the Fifties, fuels of a much higher octane rating and of considerable heat-absorption ability for internal cooling were used. Abetted by such fuels, extremely high specific power outputs were eventually attained. A typical example is the Alfa Romeo 159, which in its final version developed 425 bhp with a boost of 35 pounds per square inch.

Weighing all the factors, there is no doubt that a manufacturer will have to develop more than one type of engine to make sure he can eventually produce and install the one that performs best. Regardless of the engine he finally chooses, one assumes that the minimum power that will be required of such an engine will be 430 hp, or roughly twice the power produced by the current 1½-liter Formula One engines. The weight of a car with an engine of this output will be about 1,550 pounds at the starting line. And the power-to-weight ratio will be about 650 hp per ton, appreciably more than that of the most potent modern American sports/racing cars using big, basically stock V-8's.

With that ratio to contend with, the manufacturer's biggest problem will be to transmit the available driving force to the road. The Indianapolis Lotus, the nearest thing to a 1966 Grand Prix car, does not have this problem, because the curves of the two-and-a-half-mile Indianapolis track can be negotiated at around 145 mph, and the car will never be called on to accelerate away from a slow corner in the gears. Even with a rather high first gear (with a nine-to-one overall ratio), on which a Grand Prix car would be able to exceed 90 mph, an engine conforming to the new formula would produce a driving force of about 1,600 pounds, taking all transmission losses into account. This is higher than the starting-line weight of the car. Theoretically, therefore, even with four-wheel drive and assuming a coefficient of friction of 1.0 between the tires and the road (which is not unreasonable for modern racing tires, when road surfaces are dry), the wheels would spin, and full power could not be employed.

It must not be inferred from this that with only two driving wheels, the car would function on less than half the power. All modern racing cars have a weight bias toward the rear, and modern suspension techniques provide excellent handling with a front/rear distribution of about 40/60. Acceleration produces an additional weight transfer toward the rear, and it may be calculated that when the full acceleration potential is used, about eighty per cent of the total weight of the vehicle is borne by the rear wheels. Still presuming a coefficient of friction of 1.0, it can be estimated that for a starting-line weight of 1,550 pounds, a total of 1,240

pounds would be available for traction, leaving unused the 310 pounds carried by the front wheels.

With improvements in suspension systems, it may eventually be possible to increase the weight bias on the rear end even more without concomitant bad effects on handling. In addition, drag-strip experience indicates that coefficients of friction superior to the theoretical maximum of 1.0 can one day be assumed.

Tire improvements can also be expected to appear in the new Formula One cars, but the nature of these changes would be hard to predict. Since the new and more powerful cars will travel at higher speeds than today's Formula One models, tire manufacturers won't be able to use rubber compounds that contain greater hysteresis factors, in order to increase the grip of tires on the road, as these compounds would produce excessive heat and consequent tread failures. Increasing tire width to achieve greater contact area is another way to improve road grip, except that it does have limitations. Widening the tires tends to increase both wind and rolling resistance, and to affect the ability of a car to maneuver well in tight corners. If large contact areas exist between the tires and the road, there is a risk of aquaplaning when road surfaces are wet, which is certain to become a major problem in lightweight cars whose speed capabilities exceed 200 mph.

None of these developments—neither in tires nor suspension—could even indirectly relieve the problem of having to transmit a driving force superior to the car's own weight. The answer would appear to be four-wheel drive; however, it must be said that this configuration has a number of disadvantages built right in.

First of all, four-wheel drive is a complex mechanism that invariably makes a car bulkier and heavier. Regardless of the location of the engine—front, rear or midship—a shaft transmitting power to the non-driving end of the vehicle must pass somewhere alongside the driver. It has been suggested that two engines

could be used, one at the front and the other at the rear, each driving its own set of wheels. A similar configuration was seen at Indianapolis in 1946 in the Fageol Twin Coach Special, and in the experimental twin-engined Mini built by BMC two years ago, but it is hardly a practical solution.

The only logical way to drive all four wheels would be to link the front and rear axles in such a way that the front wheels overrun the rear ones, as is necessary in tight corners. Thus when the torque applied to the front wheels exceeds what they can take without spinning, the *excess* torque would be directed to the rear. The simplest way to achieve this would be to include a free wheel in the shaft linking the front and rear axles. But a more scientific solution is to include a limited-slip differential in the front-rear drive line (as patented by Ferguson).

Apart from making the car bulkier and heavier, the additional drive would also use up some of the power transmitted through it. A loss of five to seven per cent is probably not an exaggerated estimate, but then it should be remembered that the engine is expected to be able to exert a driving force, in low gear, of fifty pounds more than the car's starting-line weight. The excess power of about three per cent could be used to cancel out part of the transmission losses, so that the available thrust would actually be lessened by only two to four per cent. This loss would occur at low speeds when the engine develops its maximum torque in low gear.

It may also be assumed that a four-wheel-drive car would be about 100 to 200 pounds heavier than its rear-drive counterpart, a weight increase of roughly seven or eight per cent. This increase would lower the power-to-weight ratio as measured at the wheels, and result in a loss of low-speed acceleration of about the same order. Thus compared with a rear-drive car, the four-wheel-drive vehicle seems less advisable, for instead of a twenty per cent acceleration advantage, there would be no more than eleven. Small as it is, this acceleration advantage would come

41

into play only under the most favorable conditions for four-wheel drive—that is, when first gear is used and the engine delivers its maximum torque.

Outside the maximum torque range the advantage would be less, and with normal Grand Prix gearing, it would disappear altogether as soon as a higher gear is used. As speed increases, not only does the advantage of four-wheel drive decrease, but it definitely becomes a disadvantage. As soon as a competing rear-wheel-drive car comes out of the wheel-spin range, its twelve to fifteen per cent higher ratio of power to weight makes itself felt. The reason is that the four-wheel-driven car has a five to seven per cent lower transmission efficiency and a seven to eight per cent greater weight, not to mention a slightly greater frontal area.

There can be no doubt that a four-wheel-drive Grand Prix car with more than 400 hp exploding beneath its hood would run away from more conventional cars of the same power on a twisty circuit like Monaco, where the conventional car would rarely be out of the wheel-spin range. Four-wheel drive would also be an obvious asset on most circuits when made slippery by rain. But which of the known manufacturers of Grand Prix cars could afford to build a team of four-wheel-drive models just for Monaco, or to take along to all the other races in case it happened to rain? Despite its notable advantages, the limitations inherent in the four-wheel-drive configuration weigh against its becoming the rule for builders of Grand Prix cars under the new formula.

It is a known fact of race-car engineering that the less the amount of available power, the greater the distance in which full power will be used on any given circuit. From this axiom it can be seen that a very slight difference in power between two engines of the future (each with 400 to 450 hp) will be of less importance than that of today's 210 hp Grand Prix machines. Today even the best of drivers is under a handicap if an opponent of even mediocre skill happens to have ten additional horsepower at his command, because such a large proportion of most Grand Prix circuits is taken flat out. Moreover, chassis and suspensions have progressed so far that present Grand Prix cars could function with a great deal more power imposed, and it doesn't take a very sensitive foot to drive them successfully.

In a car having twice the power, and even more available, the problems involved would be entirely different. Since maximum power and maximum torque would not be employed so often, small differences in power output would not be felt as much. In most instances, it would not be a question of how much power is available, but how much of the available power can be used, and who is able to use how much. The driver thus will again become the single most important factor in a racing car's success. And the chassis and suspension designer will once more achieve prominence, because to a large extent, it will be his ability and judgment that determines the amount of power that can be used in any circumstance.

It is likely that history will repeat itself. Nearly thirty years ago, when the Grand Prix racing scene was dominated by the Nazi-sponsored Mercedes and Auto-Union teams, there was a time when the 646 hp Mercedes had an advantage of no less than 150 hp over the Auto-Union. But the latter proved as fast as the former on most circuits, beating the Mercedes several times. Lower frontal area, higher load on the driving wheels, and most important, Bernd Rosemeyer's ability to make full use of the Auto-Union's potential were sufficient to nullify the Mercedes's 150 hp advantage.

At the present stage of race-car development, and even with cars having a higher power-to-weight ratio than the German vehicles that raced under the 750-kilogram formula of 1934-37, it is conceivable that a power differential of more than twenty per cent could become immaterial. Small differences in the power delivered to driving wheels would obviously make much less difference under the future formula than they would today. The higher speeds that the new-formula cars would be capable of, and the enormous power available, would combine to present the driver an exacting task. Any new development that would enable him to concentrate even more on driving and controlling his car with greater precision would be an immense advantage.

One such development might possibly be the application of an automatic transmission, which would allow the driver to keep his hands on the wheel at all times, his mind strictly on the road —and would facilitate better controlled braking, without jerks and without the slight inconsistencies that are inevitable when heel-and-toeing. Jim Hall's Chaparral, which has nearly the same power-to-weight ratio as may be expected in future Grand Prix cars, has already proved the validity of this notion.

The use of automatic transmissions is out of the question under the present Formula One. Even if they absorbed only three or four per cent more engine power than a hand-controlled mechanical gearbox, their compensatory advantages could not offset the commensurate power loss. When horses are relatively few, none can be readily spared.

Even for the more powerful engines that are built under the new formula, production-type automatic transmissions incorporating hydraulic torque converters and epicyclic gears would probably absorb too much power, have excessive flywheel effect and be too cumbersome. The truly mechanical Hobbs transmission has already been applied, and quite successfully, by the inventor's son, David Hobbs, in a Lotus Elite some seasons ago. It is a four-speed unit with epicyclic gears, automatically or manually controlled via a hydraulic servo system that operates mechanical clutches. However, the best transmission for a racing car might be a hydrostatic type of mechanism that can be made fully automatic and fully progressive, is highly efficient, and can be made quite small and light. As far as I know, attempts to develop such transmissions for use in passenger cars have failed—partly because of low efficiency, mainly because they could not be made to work quietly enough. But in a racing car, this is the fault least likely to offend anyone.

It should also be kept in mind that a good, fully progressive automatic transmission will keep the engine working over a very narrow rpm range. If so, the shape of the torque curve becomes less important, and the designer can concentrate on increasing the maximum power, with little need for concern with what happens lower down in the range. Thus he can compensate wholly or in part for any loss of efficiency brought about by the automatic device.

Which of the four types of engines permitted under specifications of the new Formula One will give the best results? Should the drive be transmitted to two wheels or to all four? Should an automatic transmission be used, and if so, which type? These are the central and fundamental questions that racing car designers will have to answer satisfactorily for themselves before they start on the new Grand Prix cars.

Of course there will be other problems whose solution will be necessary for the completion of a concept. Brakes, tires and even chassis that are adequate for 210 hp, thousand-pound, 160 mph automobiles may not meet the requirements posed by heavier machines that have twice the horsepower—or more—and are capable of speeds in excess of 200 mph. No doubt these problems will be solved, however, and their solution will contribute to the technical progress that will ultimately be reflected in better production cars.

One cannot help feeling, though, that the new Grand Prix formula is a rather expensive way to put racing car builders and their suppliers to task, quite apart from the fact that it is based on a hardly scientific fist-and-thumb handicap: the FIA obviously hopes to broaden Formula One racing, to facilitate the use of different kinds of engines, each working on entirely differ-

ent principles. The motive is praiseworthy even if the result is not.

It should not be forgotten that the European motor sport is almost entirely dependent upon the support of oil companies that obviously expect some return on their investment—in the form of publicity, and hopefully some acclaim. Most likely the new racing cars will cost nearly twice as much as the present Formula One models, but there is little likelihood that they

will be worth twice the publicity value of today's Grand Prix race winners.

Even today, it is extremely difficult for a builder of Grand Prix cars to make a profit; thus it is easy to see why many of them do not look forward to next year with much enthusiasm, and others hope to produce sports cars that use big American modified engines. The latter would seem a much more realistic way to go motor racing at a high level of performance. ✤

HISTORY OF THE FORMULA (1906-1965)

Motor racing was not very old when manufacturers discovered that the sport could be exploited to enhance the reputation of their products. And it was around 1900 that the press awoke to the realization that motor racing could be exploited to demonstrate a nation's industrial might and engineering excellence.

Racing rules were an attempt to provide fair terms for all competitors and to accomplish something of value in the development of the automobile. Motor racing began in 1894; Grand Prix racing began twelve years later.

Prior to the arrival of GP racing, the Gordon Bennett Cup races of 1900 to 1905 were held under a formula specifying that all parts of a car must be made in its own country of origin, and that only three cars from each manufacturing nation could compete in any one race. But no limitations were applied to the technical specifications of the cars.

The national motoring organizations of Europe united in 1904 to solve the problems of international motoring and motor racing. The first internationally accepted Grand Prix formula, effective in 1906, specified a *maximum* weight, but imposed no limit on the number of entries from each country.

The 1907 formula limited both cylinder bore and fuel consumption. In 1908 the formula set down a maximum cylinder bore and a *minimum* weight. The engine displacement limit was adopted in 1914. It began at 4½ liters and was reduced to 3 liters in 1921. With the arrival of

superchargers in about 1924, the wise governors of the sport decided, in a misguided attempt to improve safety, to restrict displacement to 2 liters in 1925 and 1½ liters in 1927. The engineers overcame the restrictions of each formula by continually boosting the speeds of their cars.

There were a few wild years between 1928 and 1934. A free formula was tried, with a ten-hour-race duration. A combination of fuel consumption and weight limits was tried again. From 1934 through 1937 there was only a weight limit.

The displacement limit was reintroduced in 1938 (3 liters supercharged, 4½ liters unblown). The limits have been drastically reduced three times since then, in 1946, 1954 and 1961. But with each change, the cars have become even faster.

Under the current formula, which expires at year's end, engine displacement is restricted to 1½ liters with no supercharging, and the cars are swifter than ever. Lacking a power surplus, however, they are much less safe to drive than the 750 kg leviathans of 1937, which developed up to 645 hp.

The 1966 cars will have similar power-to-weight ratios, and no one now seems to doubt that the cars will be faster. It is still not known, however, whether the new rules are the best that could have been devised. The decision was made, and it is unimpeachable, and the controversy continues.

Photographers abound at racing events. The artist, of course, is less in evidence, for the shutter is faster than the pencil, and the substance of the race is speed. A unique exception is Walter Gotschke, a German enthusiast and artist who takes a sketchbook to the circuits. Quick sketches of racing moments as they happen are the basis of his racing paintings. Gotschke's opportunity to sketch racing in action has been curbed in recent years by his extensive work with the German automobile industry. Recently, however, he has added another dimension to his art by accepting commissions to do office and studio murals of racing scenes. His racing portrayals are famous throughout Europe. First presented to readers of this magazine in Volume II, Number 2 ("Recollections of an Enthusiast"), AUTOMOBILE *Quarterly* is again delighted to publish the art of Walter Gotschke. Exhibitions of his work— some of the paintings published here as well as many others—will take place this year at the J. Walter Thompson gallery in New York City and later at the General Motors Styling and Technical Center at Warren, Michigan. Included in this presentation is the 1955 Monaco GP and Le Mans, 1956, the latter being Gotschke's first visit to that racing classic. Accompanying the paintings are the artist's recollections of the racing moments he depicted.

RACING IMPRESSIONS

By Walter Gotschke

GRAND PRIX DE MONACO 1955
AT CASINO SQUARE

Up from the harbor like wild horses they thunder into view between the Casino and the Hôtel de Paris. Ascari leads—behind him, young Perdisa in a Maserati, a pupil studying the master. Who thought it possible that this would be Ascari's last race? Within seconds, on the same lap, he would miss the chicane and plunge into the harbor at Monte Carlo. A few months later he would die testing another car for another race. But at this moment—veiled in smoke at Casino Square—he is master.

THE TWENTY-THIRD LAP

The race of a thousand corners it's called, and the view from the steps of the railway station indicates why. The twenty-third time around the vicious downhill hairpins finds two Mercedes-Benzes—Fangio in No. 2 and Moss in No. 6—comfortably ahead of Ascari's Lancia. Hawthorn's Vanwall comes by with a broken throttle linkage. On the fiftieth lap Fangio will retire in the same spot; soon afterward Moss will be out. The victor—virtually unnoticed until the last laps—is Trintignant in a Ferrari. (Overleaf)

FANGIO, WORLD CHAMPION

I have not painted a specific race here, but rather a representation of the 1956 racing season. Juan Mañuel Fangio won his fourth world Championship. Stirling Moss on Maserati was second. It had been a long, rigorous duel. Significant, too, that year was the new four-cylinder Vanwall which won its first important race—the BRDC at Silverstone. Experts predicted success, and I painted a green Vanwall into this scene as a symbol of racing to come. The 1957 and 1958 seasons bore out my prediction.

LE MANS 1956
THE CORNER AT ARNAGE

Looking back on the corner offers a good perspective. That short straight between the two turns is frequently the scene of highly dramatic fights for position. On this lap the Ferrari and Porsche have outmaneuvered the blue Talbot and are forcing their way into the second turn in front of it. The course is rain-soaked, the air heavy with mist and the cars' exhausts a whispy circlet. Almost masked by the weather and the smoke is the Belgian Jaguar hounding the leaders from its fourth place. (At far right)

JUST BEFORE MIDNIGHT

The corner at Arnage again—this time viewing it from the approach. Here is one of the few spots providing a natural close-up of racing cars in action. A feverish air seemed to permeate the entire automobile as it was braked hard for the turn. What form! What technical beauty! The slippery road, rain and darkness served only to intensify the dramatic duel between the Moss-Collins Aston Martin (No. 8) and the Ecurie Ecosse Jaguar (No. 4). In a few moments the Jaguar was to take the lead.

MORNING

The seesaw battle between Aston Martin and Jaguar continued through the night. Around four o'clock the former held a tenuous nineteen-second lead. But as day began to break, the Jaguar spirited ahead, and now along the straight to Mulsanne it enjoys a lead of more than one minute over the Aston Martin. The low morning mist is rolling in; headlights pierce through it. From behind, the cars appear as guided shots along an open road. The race is half over. The sky is becoming light.

RECALLING THE BEGINNING

After long hours at roadside watching the Jaguar-Aston Martin duel, my mind slipped back to the start of the race. The setting was almost like that for a wide-screen movie theatre. Moss's famed sprint across the road had succeeded again, and the Aston Martin led off the procession, closely followed by the Ecurie Ecosse Jaguar. That was Saturday, a few seconds after 4:00 p.m. Twenty-four hours later, the checkered flag was lowered for the Ecurie Ecosse Jaguar. In second place—the Aston Martin. (Overleaf)

IN THE PITS

Not all the drama of racing happens on the road. In a race such as Le Mans the pit stop is a theatrical vignette in itself. My station during the race and my roof when it rained were the Porsche pits, a comfortable observation post until there was a driver change. Then like lightning everything started to move. Von Trips, out of the car in a flash, briefs team manager von Hanstein. Team engineer Hild oversees refueling, as von Frankenberg moves to take the wheel. Then the race is on once more.

EPITAPH FOR THE TIN GOOSE

by ALEX TREMULIS

Little more than a year ago, AUTOMOBILE Quarterly *outlined the ordeal by trial of the late Preston Tucker, a man of uncommon vision who dared attempt transforming his dream car into a reality. In this issue we focus on the car itself and the story behind the Tucker Torpedo. It was a dream car in the purest sense, for it embodied the tangible aspects of one man's ideal. Preston Tucker sought to build an automobile that was not only powerful and efficient but comfortable and safe, revolutionary in concept and free from pre-World War II clichés. Nearly two decades have passed since the Tucker Corporation was formed, but even so, many innovations built into the Tucker car have only recently found their way into American passenger car design. Only fifty Tuckers were ever built, and fewer still remain in existence. A small knot of enthusiasts continue to be faithful, cherishing the car and its memory, but few could be as passionate in their devotion to it as those who played a part in its creation. Among this group is the man responsible for styling the Tucker. What follows herewith are his recollections of two years spent on the car's development, a period he considers one of the most exciting of his styling career.*

I shall always refer to the passing of the Tucker Corporation as a great American tragedy. I have no doubt that if Preston Tucker had succeeded in building what he was sure was the world's finest motorcar, we would all be driving today the kind of automobile that we shall have to wait until perhaps 1970 to see. Such would have been Tucker's impact on the auto industry if the car he envisioned had been manufactured successfully.

But unfortunately the car that began as a dream ended in ignominy, as Preston Tucker waged a four-month-long court fight to clear himself of charges of having conspired to defraud the stockholders and dealers who had invested in the promotion of his car. Not unexpectedly, I was subpoenaed by the court as a witness in the trial. I was called in to see Robert Downing, the assistant prosecuting attorney, who interrogated me at length, hoping to persuade me to admit that the name Tin

Goose implied that the Tucker was a hodgepodge because it had been built from an old Oldsmobile. I was adamant in insisting that Tin Goose, the nickname we used in the shop, was a form of endearment, and there was nothing in our use of the epithet to imply that the car was a pile of junk, as he was intimating. I reminded him that one of the most illustrious airplanes of all times, Bill Stout's Ford Trimotor, had also been called Tin Goose—and also out of affection and respect.

Further, I explained to him that I had chopped up a 1942 Oldsmobile only so it could be used as an interior buck, allowing me to establish the extremely critical door hinging required by the fact that our door openings extended into the roof structure. I had intended to build the first Tin Goose out of clay, but there was none available for this purpose immediately after the war. I told Downing that I had tried to buy or borrow the clay from the Briggs Manufacturing Company, but that they refused, coveting it as though it were priceless and irreplaceable.

I could have built the car out of wood, except that we did not have pattern-shop facilities at that time. The car was intended as a styling mock-up, and we chose to make it in metal because we had a group of superior metal craftsmen available to us. Had I known that the name Tin Goose would be used as an instrument to pound nails into the coffin of the Tucker Corporation, I would have personally carved the automobile out of marble.

I was called to the stand—as prosecution witness number thirteen, unluckily. Mr. Downing examined me, opening with some questions relevant to advertising art and to the way one goes about designing an automobile. Then he led into what was to be his final question: what did I call the car? "The Tin Goose," I told him, suppressing a smile, for I anticipated that his next question would be, "Why?" My answer would surely have punctured this phase of the prosecution's case. Unhappily, the question was not asked. I was dismissed from the stand, anguished and frustrated.

Another witness who had been called to the stand that day, a disgruntled Tucker employee, had labeled the car a monstrosity. Evening newspapers chose to combine our two statements, and I found to my dismay that front pages contained my picture beneath headlines that read, in effect, "Tucker Car Called Monstrosity—Stylist Labels Car Tin Goose."

My testimony represented but a fragment of the prosecution's case against Preston Tucker. In all, seventy-two government witnesses were paraded before the jury (see Volume II, Number 4). Not even then would Preston take the stand. His attorneys advised against it, insisting that there could be no defense when no offense had been committed. When the case was finally closed, the jury deliberated for seventeen hours, seven minutes, and ultimately concurred that Tucker and his aides should be acquitted. Thus despite the reams of "evidence" presented against him, Preston Tucker was declared innocent of all charges, but by then his dream had been shattered. And before he was able to revive it—a man as determined as Tucker could never have given up—he was struck by a fatal illness. He died the day after Christmas, 1956.

Preston Tucker was an extraordinary man, a man of many facets, and most of all, a man whose drive and enthusiasm were such that everyone around him was caught up in the whirlwind he created. There were times when I looked upon him as a mathematical moron, at other times an immature businessman ill equipped to hack his way through the jungle of modern commerce. And often he seemed to me just a brash, overgrown kid with a passion for automobiles.

Actually he possessed all these idiosyncrasies, in some measure, and a great many virtues as well. He was a combination of four great men with whom I have been associated in my career in the aircraft and automotive industries. Periodically he reminded me of Roy Faulkner, the sales managerial genius of Pierce-Arrow and later the president of Auburn-Cord-Duesenberg. With compassion for youthful creativity, Faulkner encouraged a young art student, Phil Wright, to whom he gave *carte blanche* for the design of what proved to be one of the world's most advanced automobiles, the Silver Arrow of 1933. Often, Tucker evinced qualities I recall in Theodore von Karman, father of the supersonic breakthrough, whose stimulating guidance and inspiring dedication to pure research left a contribution to the science of aeronautics that may never be equaled by another man in our time. Preston's devotion to and relentless pursuit of perfection was matched only by the legendary August Duesenberg, who also lived by the conviction that he was building the finest of all motorcars. Lastly, he reminded me of John Tjaarda, a tireless exponent of the rear-engined automobile, whose enthusiasm for the principle reduced every other configuration to the status of a Napoleonic coach.

Time after time, when a major styling decision had to be made, Preston deferred to me, invariably cautioning me, "Just remember that we have a boss bigger than all of us and that's the automobile. Do what you have to do, but be sure it's right for the car." The authority he gave me was the answer to a stylist's prayer. It was a kind of utopia, but more akin to that enjoyed by a scientist at work in the Soviet Union, I'm afraid. Like the latter, I knew that if successful I would see myself crowned with glory. And, conversely, if I failed, Tucker would doubtless have me pilloried, for *I* would be solely to blame for any faults in the styling of the car. This was certainly a perilous responsibility, but it is one that a stylist must be willing to accept.

The tragedy of the trial of Preston Tucker was that his car was never defended. Had Preston taken the stand, the vehicle's most interesting design details would have been brought to light. As advanced as these were at the time, all had been realized in the car Tucker produced.

The Tucker car was certainly unique, and in ways that combined to make an important contribution to the art of automotive design. Even more significant was the fact that those of us involved in the project had literally started from scratch. It was as if Detroit had emerged from the war in rubble, its plants and tooling completely demolished. If this had actually occurred, and American factories had been leveled by repeated bombings, Detroit designers would have been totally uninhibited, free from the strictures of inherited prewar specifications. Fortunately continental America was untouched by World War II, and at the close of hostilities, was in a decidedly healthy economic state. But unfortunately, to meet the unprecedented postwar demand for product, automakers hauled out their prewar dies, and with little variation, turned out cars that were only mildly facelifted versions of the cars most people had just worn out.

With no prewar models to guide us, or to restrict us either, we at Tucker sincerely believed that in starting fresh, we had a tremendous advantage over our Detroit competition, and that furthermore, since we had no set precedents to be concerned with, we could prepare to build a car whose engine was in the rear. We regarded the drive shaft of contemporary cars as a relic of marine engineering, referring to it as a propeller shaft. Its only purpose, it seemed to us, was to commit the felony of robbing a car of interior space and forcing passengers to ride on top of a vibrating drive shaft that had to be tranquilized by a myriad of universal joints.

A rear-engined car would give us the technical advantage of being able to eliminate the so-called camel's hump; it would also increase interior seating dimensions proportionately and allow us to lower the overall height of our car to sixty inches and still provide four more inches of interior height than our nearest competitor. The middle passenger in the front or rear seat, the man we referred to as the forgotten man, would no longer have to straddle an intrusive hump. And we could now lower the floor to a level nine inches above the ground, instead of the customary fourteen or fifteen inches, which our competitors were forced to maintain, and still have adequate ground clearance (which we believed should be a minimum of eight inches).

To accomplish this, of course, we would have to eliminate the X member, which would be no loss because its only justification was to embrace the sins of the drive shaft. With no X member and no drive shaft to contend with, we could simply run our structure transversely under the seats. To further simplify the frame, we eliminated the rear wheel kickup by resorting to parallel arms in the front suspension and rear trailing arms in the rear suspension. By carefully revising our early styling dimensions, we seized the opportunity to make both outboard and inboard frame rails interchangeable. We were delighted to find that we not only surpassed the sturdiness of the frame of the 1948 Oldsmobile—which was the most rigid, according to our tests of competing frames—but we also shaved some eighty-five pounds from the weight of the Olds frame in the process.

Another advantage offered by this unique interchangeability of frame rails was that by controlling the plan view styling dimensions, we could also arrive at interchangeable front and rear seat cushions—which could be switched at the same time a car owner decided to rotate his tires. The telltale marks of wear and tear on the driver's seat telegraphed the age of cars in the late Forties, the time of the mohair dynasty before vinyl was king, with the result that the cars would suffer a greater depreciation if and when they were to be resold.

Our concern with design interchangeability prompted us to conceive a single interchangeable center pillar. This permitted us to anchor the door hinges in the front and rear areas of the body, where we could control body rigidity and at the same time foment greater ease of entry and egress for back-seat passengers.

A question that was often asked of us during the early days of the car's development was how we could hope to compete with the giants of Detroit with respect to tooling and manufacturing. One answer was that the sheer simplicity of our design approach contributed savings of millions of dollars in extensive tooling. This simplicity was possible because of the perfect coordination between the engineering and styling departments during the product planning stage. Naturally there were differences, and inevitably, compromises. One of these that comes to mind was the battle of inches. The sales department and some members of the engineering staff were convinced that the car should be sixty-four inches tall. I felt that fifty-six inches would be acceptable, since the floor of the car was to be only nine inches off the road. The sixty-four-inch height seemed ridiculous—exceeding by some four inches the interior dimensions of the Cadillac and Packard, both of which were already auditoriums of interior spaciousness, to my way of thinking.

The people in sales refused to back down. They staked out patches of tape at sixty-four-inch heights throughout our offices, hoping, no doubt, to educate my eye and convince me that the height they wanted was not unreasonable. The day I found myself staring at a strip of tape placed sixty-four inches high in the washroom, I decided that it was time to get a decision from Preston Tucker. He settled the question by establishing the height of the crash pad in the interior mockup. He wanted the crash pad high enough for passengers to be able to duck into what he called the "basement" in times of emergency. Tucker's prescribed crash-pad location made my argument untenable. As he did not wish his styling and sales departments to continue squabbling, he made both sides compromise, and the height of the car was set at sixty inches.

Preston's high regard for safety was driven home to us fully when he invited the entire engineering group to a luncheon to listen to an eminent Detroit plastic surgeon who was waging a one-man crusade for automobile safety. I recall that just as dessert was being served, the doctor began narrating a color-slide presentation that showed accident victims who had been brought into hospital emergency rooms. As each picture was projected, he described with unfailing accuracy the styling of the gash marks on each victim's face, and compared them to the offending styling objects, such as the radio grille of a particular car or the heater knob. It was a distasteful show, and the cause of a lot of uneaten desserts, but it made an impact on all of us. We immediately revised our thinking, relative to the interior of the car.

Out went our ten-inch window-lift handles, which Preston himself had designed. He had sought to eliminate the cumbersome cranking motions required to raise and lower windows—by substituting a simple bar that moved sixty degrees up or down, upon pressure from a passenger's hand. We now had to incorporate the door handle and window lift into one organized unit—a recessed chrome handle, with a one-and-a-quarter-inch knob for the window lift, which pivoted around a six-inch flush bezel. We then transferred all driver control knobs to the left side of the instrument panel and arranged to have crash padding around the entire circumference of the car's interior and across the back of the front seat. The crash basement was now to be covered with one full inch of slow-deceleration rubber, and glove compartments were to be moved into the door panels. The rear-view mirror was to be of plexiglass and silver plated for reflection, and it was to be mounted on a breakaway standard that would leave a flush mounting in the event of an accident. The windshield was to be floated in sponge rubber and so installed that it would pop out when a force of 100 pounds per square inch was applied to it from within. According to our automobile medical laboratory, pressures of more than 125 pounds per square inch constituted a brain concussion.

Another area on which a great deal of developmental activity was focused was the Tucker steering gear. Because of the car's rear-engine location, steering forces were extremely low. It was a unique experience. in those days before power steering, to park a Tucker car. With one or two fingers on the wheel spoke, one could spin the steering wheel like a roulette wheel. This was indeed a new sensation, and frankly most of us didn't like it at all. We insisted that the car should have greater road feel. We accomplished this by changing the ratio so that it required two and a half to three turns of the wheel to go from lock to lock. We now had steering maneuverability in the best sports car tradition. Under violent skid conditions, one could make an instantaneous steering correction by grasping the steering hub, and with a twist of the wrist, go from lock to lock in a fraction of a second. The effortless steering was due in part to the design of the wheels. Preston insisted on the use of disk brakes in order to place the kingpin location in the centerline of the wheel itself—a forward-looking approach, for this is exactly what GM did on the Firebird III (one of the most sophisticated dream cars of all time) some ten years later.

All this development work on the steering mechanism had one ulterior purpose. Preston Tucker believed that the steering shaft was the greatest cause of serious injury in auto accidents, and he hoped to eliminate it entirely by 1950. At such time, the steering wheel was to be cantilevered off the crash pad and would be collapsible under impact. Steering control would be effected through a flexible cable or a dual system of hydraulic lines.

Braking power of the Tucker car was as extraordinary as its steering. As a result of its engine being located in the rear, the car maintained its equilibrium even under maximum braking conditions. In an ordinary front-engined car, under such conditions, the weight shift from rear to front would result in the front wheels' absorbing seventy-five per cent and the rear wheels the remaining twenty-five per cent of the braking forces required to stop. It had been hoped that the Tucker car could be braked from a speed of 90 mph to a dead stand in 240 feet (less than half the normal distance in an average car). This was an unreasonable expectation and was never fulfilled, but I feel certain that with today's advanced cohesion of tires, we could have exceeded that requirement.

As a further consideration for safety, we conducted a survey to determine how the public would react to the installation of safety belts on our car. Racing drivers were consulted, first of all, revealing a wide difference of opinion. One of them, Rex Mays, offered us little encouragement, assuring us that in the event of a roll-over, he preferred to abandon the car. Ironically, this great driver might still be alive if he had not been thrown from his car in his last ride at the Los Angeles Speedway in 1949.

Although the safety value of seat belts was obvious to those of us designing the car, the Tucker sales department maintained that the presence of safety belts would imply that the automobile was dangerous. We interviewed airline hostesses who admitted they had trouble getting passengers to fasten safety belts during take-offs and landings. And in discussing passenger safety with a major airline executive, we were told, "If we put a parachute under each seat, this would imply that an element of danger existed and would so terrify the passengers that they would file out of the airplane and seek the closest railroad terminal in an exodus that would look like the evacuation of Dunkirk." In one of my more playful moods I suspended two football helmets on coil springs from the roof of our seating mock-up and jokingly told Preston that I had found the ultimate solution. Preston was not at all amused and threatened to make me attend the funeral of every person killed in a Tucker if I failed to make it the safest car in the world.

At times his obsession with safety reached some impracticable extremes. For a while he was insistent that the frame of the car taper to a point at the front, so that in a fifty per cent head-on collision, the car would glance off, and if two Tuckers happened to collide in even a one hundred per cent head-on, the glance-off would also be complete. We finally convinced Preston that though reducing the frontal area would provide added protection in some types of accidents, passengers would be more vulnerable to injury in many others.

Preston was not so easily dissuaded from his desire to have a periscope, however, for he felt certain that such a device was essential to expanding maximum rear visibility. We investigated several proposals, each of which would have increased production costs substantially, but cost was not the only deterrent. The problems of integrating a periscope were such that instead of designing a periscope for the car, we would have had to design a car around the periscope. I delivered the *coup de grâce* by suggesting that by eliminating the rear window, we could compensate for the cost of the periscope. Eventually I proposed a slightly V-shaped mirror that gave us a beautiful 180-degree rear-view panorama, and the periscope talk ended.

The relevance of vision to safety was emphasized to us by our medical department. We were told, for example, that everyone drives one mile in ten totally blind, because the average man blinks once every six seconds or approximately ten times in a minute. His "blindness" is enhanced by the fact that his eyes must make a sharp transition in focus from, say, 300 yards to twenty inches every time he views the speedometer on the instrument panel. The latter fact prompted us to develop a speedometer that would be mounted in the hood-ornament position and would allow the driver to keep his eyes on the road at all times. Then, realizing that a driver would have to shift his focus to the rear-view mirror now and then, we resolved to put the fuel gauge and warning lights above the rear window where they would be visible constantly in the mirror.

The prototype hood-position speedometer was an astounding success to

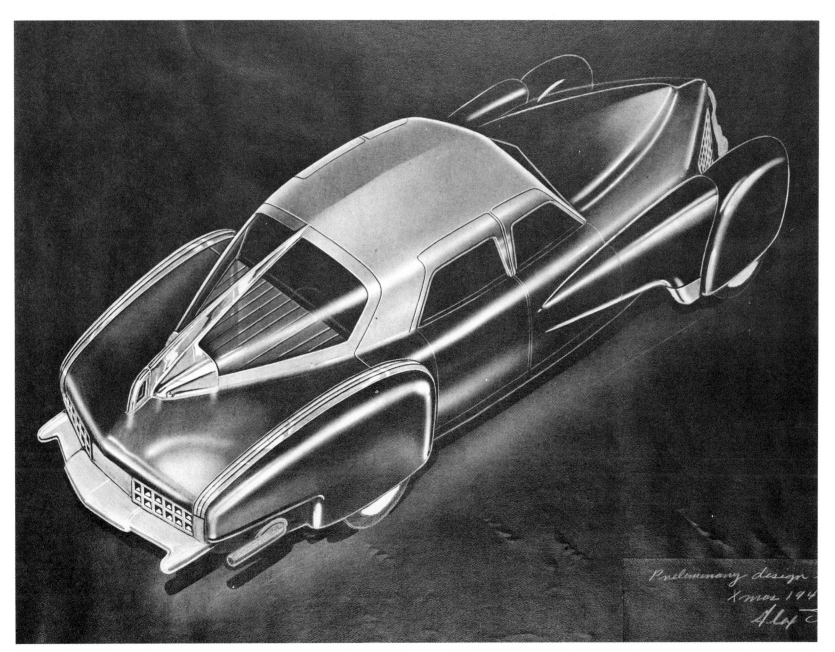

Preliminary design
Xmas 194

In its development, the Tucker car assumed many shapes until the final design was determined. Here is one of the author's first drawings, presented as a "preliminary" but received with such enthusiasm that Alex Tremulis was immediately asked to become the Tucker Corporation's chief stylist.

all who viewed it from the driver's seat. However, we received tremendous resistance from the sales people, who accused us of stripping the interior of so much that is usually considered ornamental as well as functional that the end result was something akin to the sterility of a padded cell. There were other problems, too, mechanical as well as theoretical, associated with the outside speedometer. For example, every time we opened the hood (which was the Tucker's trunk lid), some ten feet of speedometer cable whipped out and did a virtual snake dance. There was no way to combat this, so armed with war-surplus gun sights, rheostats and radio dials, we began making experiments to project the image of the speedometer-reading onto the windshield itself. As far as the sales department was concerned, this approach contributed further to making the car interior sterile and bland. So we compromised by mounting the speedometer in the conventional position in front of the driver; somehow we arrived at the solution of making the speedometer numbers at least five-eighths of an inch high. Preston was still receptive to our thinking, however, and assured us we would live to fight another day.

Another controversial detail brought about by Preston's zeal for safety was the center-mounted "Cyclops" headlight that was to turn as the wheels turned to guide the car around curves and corners. Several states had laws that prohibited the "Cyclops," for one thing. But we were able to satisfy these restrictions by designing a cover for the light, ornamented with a Tucker crest, which could be applied wherever it was required by law. One problem that we were never able to solve was the center beam's consistent failure to penetrate the outboard light beams, although admittedly it did intensify the light area in the direction of the steered wheels. As we had no intention of giving up the center light, it was decided that in the evolutionary refinement of future models, we would place the outboard lights under a glass shield, as on today's Jaguar XK-E, and further, that we would make *these* two lights steerable and the center light a straight-ahead fixed beam.

From the foregoing, it might be inferred that the development of the Tucker was a gradual process, with ample time for experiment, trial and error. Nothing could be farther from the truth. In fact, I am reasonably sure that it was one of the fastest design jobs ever done for a production car. From the time I first became associated with the Tucker Corporation, the pace of work was frenzied, and the pressure at many times unbearable. It was the week before Christmas, 1946, that I first communicated with Preston Tucker and requested an appointment. When I saw him a week later, he told me he could give me just fifteen minutes as he had a luncheon engagement.

Those fifteen minutes stretched to three hours, as it happened, and by the time I left Preston's office I had a styling-study contract in my hand. The next five days were spent exploring themes and recommendations that I had discussed with him at our meeting. At about 7 p.m.,

New Year's Eve, Preston paid me a visit at the office of a product design firm in the Field Building, Chicago, where I was then working. He was on his way to a party. I had made some sketches, and when I showed them to Preston, he said simply, "That's it." Nobody could have been more surprised than I; so far as I was concerned, the sketches were just preliminaries, but Tucker insisted that first thoughts are always best. "The trouble with you stylists," he said, "is that you never know when to stop." Tucker told my wife to tear up my styling-study contract, for I was no longer a consultant, that as of New Year's Eve I was chief stylist for the Tucker Corporation. It was a pleasant way to start the new year, and thinking back, I realize that Tucker was right in having a high regard for first thoughts. At least ninety per cent of the design ideas I showed him on New Year's Eve found their way into the production car.

Tremulis (at far right) and his brilliant design staff labored long and meticulously to refine each detail of the Tucker Torpedo's wooden miniature.

On New Year's Day I conferred again with Preston. I now insisted that the Tucker car be fully aerodynamic and that it express my design philosophy. Further, I told him that if he didn't let me design the car my way, I would return to the aircraft profession where people really liked my work. Reflecting back, I realize how brash I was then. But I had remembered Theodore von Karman's advice to those of us in the design branch of Aircraft Laboratory Wright Field during World War II. He counseled us not merely to talk about something we believed in, but to *do it*. And as a fillip to drive home his point, he would say, "Remember, the meek shall inherit nothing."

Preston Tucker's advice, on that first day of 1947, was similar, but there was more urgency in it. "Grab the ball and run with it," he told me, "but just make sure the car doesn't look as if it were frightened by an airplane. I want it ready for paint in sixty days!"

"Sixty days!" I exclaimed. "It'll take me at least sixty days for a clay model."

"Who said clay? I've got the best metal man in the world waiting for you. Go! Go! Go!"

Tucker wasn't kidding—about being in a hurry or about the capability of his staff. He had indeed assembled a great wealth of talent, all under one manufacturing roof. Herman Ringling was the sheet-metal maestro. Remember the ill-fated Stutz Black Hawk of 1928? (See Volume III, Number 3.) Ringling had pounded out that vehicle for Frank Lockhart's Land Speed Record attempt, movable fender fairings and all, in just thirty days. He had built seven out of the ten front-wheel-drive Ford-Miller Indy cars of 1935. And he was known for his ability to repair a car that had gone over the wall two days before the 500-mile race and have it on the starting line in prime paint on race day.

The first Tucker engine, an enormous 589-cubic-inch affair, was set cross-wise on the overhang between the two independently sprung rear wheels.

Despite the safety factors inherent in the Tucker's uncluttered dashboard, the sales force took a dim view of what seemed to them a "barren" look.

63

In addition to Ringling there was Al McKenzie, top racing mechanic for the Horace Dodge boats, who could bench-engineer anything; Bill Burns, who with tremendous aircraft know-how, designed the Heath Silver Bullet, which flew 168 mph on only 40 hp and was lightweight enough for him to carry on his back; Gene Haustine, who could put anything together, test it, dismantle it, smash it, and who earned his stripes going over the wall at Indy; Joe Lencki, technical adviser on fuel injection and suspension units. These were the leaders, with a carefully picked group of craftsmen under them, and all revered Preston Tucker.

Once assembled, the Tucker team pounded metal, welded frames, unwelded them, made mistakes, corrected them, scrapped everything, started again from scratch. Sundays or Tuesdays, it made no difference, when each of us was working 400 to 440 hours a month! One of our men collapsed. In a panic, we rushed him to the hospital. Two hours later, I was called to the telephone—to hear the voice of an angry doctor remonstrating me: "What on earth are you people doing over there? There's nothing wrong with this man pathologically. He's just suffering from malnutrition and complete exhaustion." I used to look at Herman Ringling, then in his early sixties, and think he would never live to see the car completed. But he made it. We all did—not in sixty days, as Preston had wished, but in a hundred, which was remarkable, even so. When the Tin Goose rolled out in its pearlescent maroon, we knew we had a winner. It was worth the sweat and tears we had shed in making it. Call Preston Tucker what you will, he was a prime mover, the force that motivated us all. No one will ever convince me that Tucker wasn't trying to build an automobile!

On June 19, 1947, more than five thousand persons crowded into the Tucker plant on Chicago's South Side to view the Tucker car for the first time. The group gathered in the vast assembly room, and while a host of speakers extolled the virtues of the new car, mechanics backstage were putting finishing touches to it and making necessary final adjustments. When the curtains were finally pulled back and the car was revealed, the audience rose to its feet and cheered. And the cheering swelled in the months to come. Visiting dignitaries from all over the world came to see the car. Manolete, the greatest bullfighter of them all, had to have the first car in Mexico, he said. I was to be his guest, and he would even dedicate a bull to the automobile. General Jonathan Wainwright, hero of Corregidor and Bataan, wanted to be the first Tucker owner in Texas. Jack Barclay, the world's largest retailer of Rolls-Royce cars, called the car "the most beautiful thing this side of the Atlantic. I didn't think the Americans were capable of such things."

As orders for the car flowed in, it began to seem that we would somehow have to deliver at least 300,000 cars the first year, even though the Tucker plant's production capacity was one-third that number. In a few short months the 300-man Tucker team grew to 2,200. Hundreds of engineers, draftsmen, tooling experts and pattern makers were swarming into Chicago. To attract many of these people, we had to offer them double and sometimes triple the salaries they were getting. Somehow it didn't bother us. We were certain that once the automobile was launched, all would be well with us. Even the styling section had an expansion program. Philip Egan, a tremendously talented young enthusiast who now heads his own design firm, joined me as my assistant. He contributed immeasurably to solving the endless number of details and surface adjustments involved in transferring the conceptual Tin Goose into a production car.

I had always felt that a woman's touch was needed in designing the interior of a car. Thus Audrey Moore, who had worked with the Studebaker styling staff for Raymond Loewy, became head of all interior styling on the Tucker. Once staffed, we were ready to start refining our Tin Goose, prior to tooling it for production.

Although Preston Tucker's immediate concern was the financing of his company and the production of his car, he had his eyes on the future at the selfsame time. Hoping to develop a gas turbine engine for use in future Tucker cars, Preston hired Secundo Campini, an Italian scientist and inventor. I don't know if Campini was the world's foremost jet authority, as Preston claimed; however, history entitles him to the benefit of the doubt because of the epochal flight of the first turbine airplane, the Campini Caproni, in 1932. A Campini turbine was to be tried out in a Land Speed Record vehicle that Preston hoped would return possession of the record to the United States.

The Tucker turbine car was never built, but speed was to remain a vital part of the company's existence and was to be the crucible for all our advance concepts of engineering. For the 1950 racing season a team of six Grand Prix cars based on the Miller four-wheel drive, rear-engine concept, with fully enclosed aerodynamic coachwork, was to be captained by Ralph Hepburn, a fifty-one-year-old racing veteran. Preston had deplored the automotive industry's attitude toward racing in Europe. Thus Hepburn was to amass the greatest racing talents in the country, and with the Red, White and Blue emblazoned on the sides of their cars, the team was to challenge the world's finest racing vehicles on their home grounds. Unfortunately, Hepburn died in the crash of his high-speed Novi while practicing for the Indianapolis race. It was Sunday, May 16, 1948, two weeks before the thirty-second running of the speed classic. His untimely death curtailed our enthusiasm, and our racing program was ultimately suspended.

Ralph was a great man, and his passing was a great loss to the Tucker Corporation, as he had constantly given us the benefit of his technical experience. Ironically, England's Colin Chapman, in stating his theories of racing car design, recently predicted that the race car of the future would be a rear-engined, four-wheel drive Lotus-type vehicle—in essence a sophisticated version of the Miller special that Preston had bought and entered in the Indianapolis 500 in 1946.

Our visits to Indy in 1948 were not all the result of our interest in racing. We had no proving ground on which to test the first of our fifty pilot models coming off the line, so we made all our high-speed runs on the highway from Chicago to Kankakee, Illinois. We were a continual source of embarrassment to state troopers, whose 105 mph squad cars were being left in our dust. Our problem was to beat the troopers to the company gates. Once we were inside, our guards would slam the gates on them. Withdrawing in defeat, they would plead repeatedly that we find ourselves a race track for our trials.

Since we were breaking the law and did not wish to be prosecuted for it, we rented the Indianapolis Speedway for our final shakedown runs. We sent eight Tuckers to "the brickyard" and ran high-speed tests for a month. We knew that if the Tucker had any oversteering tendencies, we would surely find them at the speedway.

Actually, we did make a number of modifications there. Our rubber torsialastic suspensions were a bit too soft, and after two or three hundred miles at better than 100 mph speeds, the cars would squat two or three inches closer to the ground. (Standing fifty-eight inches tall, they were just beautiful, by the way.) Rubber company representatives told us not to worry, that they would come up with the right rubber compound very soon.

To give the Tucker extra cornering power, we installed sway bars, with the result that Eddie Offutt, our chief experimental engineer, was going through all the corners at 105 mph and was consistently hitting 117 mph (corrected speedometer) on the back stretch. This performance can be compared with the fact that eleven years prior I had ridden several hundred miles with Ab Jenkins in a supercharged Cord during a twenty-four-hour run for the Stevens Trophy. Ab's fastest lap *ever* was 91 mph. With due respect to the Cord, which cornered magnificently on the Indy track, I must point out that by the time Tucker cars were being tested, the track had been paved on the back stretch where Ab had been forced to contend with two brick straightaways. This had cost the Cord 4 mph in lap speed. Considering that both cars weighed the same, had the same frontal area and were closely related in terms of power output (166 hp for the Tucker, 175 for the Cord), we could still lap 10 mph faster under similar track conditions.

Reflecting back, I am certain that the Tucker's exceptional cornering ability was the result of its being truly the first of the wide-track cars. Automobiles of that day had inherited the fifty-six-inch tread, a dimension handed down from early Roman racing chariots whose wheels were spaced the width of two horses standing side by side. The Tucker front

tread was sixty-three inches, the rear sixty-five, a width that has yet to be exceeded.

After the speed tests came the acceleration tests conducted by Warren Rice, designer of the R3 automatic transmission, which was planned as our production transmission. We ran zero to 60 mph in ten seconds, zero to 80 mph in fifteen seconds, zero to 90 mph in twenty-two seconds, and zero to 100 mph in thirty-three seconds consistently. The fastest car in America then, a 150 hp luxury car at that, required twenty-two seconds to go from zero to 80 mph.

One early morning, during the test period at Indy, the Tucker had its baptism of fire as a safety vehicle. Eddie Offutt had lapped the track several times at better than 100 mph. Rather than change the right rear tire—which could normally survive only four or five laps at that speed without producing oversteering tendencies—he reversed his direction, now circling the track clockwise. Eddie was really stabbing it that day: 112 mph on the short north straight. Later he said he thought he heard the engine backfire, and he didn't think he could get through the turn without power if the engine failed. He hit the brakes hard and took the car into the infield just as one of the tubeless tires we had been testing for production let go. The car did a grand "razzoo" on the wet grass and rolled over three times at more than 80 mph, then landed on its wheels. A flash of panic struck the onlookers in the moments of silence that followed. Then Offutt stepped out, his only injury a bump on one knee, which the gearshift bracket had struck when the car rolled over. More important, even, than the minor extent of Eddie's injuries was the fact that the Tucker's windshield had popped out, upon impact, just as the advertisements said it would! After the blown tire had been changed, the car was returned to the pit area under its own power.

The Tucker's high-speed performance (120 mph) was the result of its inherently aerodynamic efficiency. We had a considerable advantage over front-engined cars. The internal drag of air entering an engine compartment through the radiator core was eliminated by placing the engine in the rear; thus the front-end sheet metal offered excellent air penetration qualities. The air intake ducts in the rear fenders were designed to channel and direct air to the rear-mounted radiator core, where it was exhausted through the rear-mounted grille. The chop-off of the rear also contributed to turbulence that fomented additional scavenging of the engine-compartment heat at speed.

The low floor height of the Tucker made possible a smooth, functional underpan that eliminated the turbulence effect of exposed members and chassis components that were a constant source of drag on conventional motorcars. The roof tapered in two directions to reduce high-lift forces. Coasting tests indicated that the car's coefficient of drag was as low as .30, whereas a conventional postwar car was on the order of .52. The Tucker car consumed 52 hp of aerodynamic drag at 100 mph, as compared to an average of 90 to 95 hp for conventional cars of that day.

The original engine that Tucker proposed was to be made of aluminum with a 589-cubic-inch displacement and a five-inch bore and stroke. Its valves were to be actuated by hydraulic lines, in order to eliminate the valve train as we know it today and assure greater silence. On each end of the engine there was to be a torque converter, which supplied final power to the wheels. It idled at 100 rpm, actually pushed the car 50 mph at only 500 rpm, and would turn up a maximum of 1,200 to 1,300 rpm at a theoretical 130 mph. Because of its extremely low rpm, the engine was expected to have lifetime reliability. It was truly a masterpiece of simplicity in concept, but had several serious shortcomings that would have required years of developmental work to redeem.

First of all, it was difficult to start the engine, as all the valves remained shut until actuated by the hydraulic pump. We finally had to resort to using a twenty-four volt electrical system, in the days of the six-volt system, in order to start the engine. The torque converters also required more development, and a means for reversing the car had to be worked out. The body program by now had reached the point where we were tooling for production. Since the engine we were working on would obviously not be ready in time, Tucker was desperate to find another powerplant. Aircooled Motors, a Syracuse, New York, firm, had developed a six-cylinder, 335-cubic-inch engine for use in helicopters. The engine had passed the rigid 150-hour full-rated power test that the Air Force had specified. Under normal test conditions the average automobile could survive only forty or fifty hours of such punishment.

The late Carl Doman, who had developed the engine, was a recognized world authority on the air-cooled art. He believed that because of the war, the air-cooled concept had progressed so much that it would be wholly reliable as an auto engine. Preston agreed, but was afraid that a segment of the public would recall the air-cooled Franklin of 1905, which had been built especially for the Vanderbilt Cup, but which failed even to qualify in the elimination race. Thus the Tucker engine was converted to a water-cooled machine that developed 150 hp with more than 300 pounds torque, and weighed 300 pounds dry. This engine, redesigned by Tucker's chief engineer Ben Parsons, was a flat six with three cylinders opposing the other three. It was built primarily of aluminum with chromium cylinder bores. Eventually it was to have had a unique fuel injection system and a cooling system sealed right in. Like the original Doman engine, it had a 335-inch capacity.

In my design of the frame I had allowed enough rear overhang to accommodate the engine. This configuration was a boon to cost reduction in the manufacture of the car, and for the consumer, would bring forth unprecedented simplicity in maintenance. To the engine we would now attach a cross member, which could be bolted to the frame during the last phase of final production. Thus by the removal of four large bolts, and with a quick disconnect of the umbilical cord and its electrical components, an engine could be removed and replaced by two men in fifteen minutes. The speed of this operation was demonstrated often to weekend visitors to the Tucker plant.

A new production technique had thus been born. It would facilitate the merging of body, engine and drive line in a relatively simple fashion on the final-assembly line—with no need for workmen to crawl inside, outside or underneath the car to connect the various elements as the car moved down the line. Even more significant, at least to the consumer, was the fact that a car owner with a "sick" engine could drive to a dealer, exchange his engine for a loaner (just as he might get a loaner battery) and come back for his engine some days later, after it had been repaired or reconditioned by the factory.

The Tucker was not only new, but revolutionary, fully ten years ahead of its time. We knew that no Detroit manufacturer would dare build a car as streamlined as ours, for fear someone might associate it with the Chrysler Airflow. Not only in styling was the car ahead of its time, but certainly in engineering, and many of its refinements have since been adapted to other production cars. The Tucker's exhaust pipes —there were six of them—were integrated into the rear bumper. Each wheel was independently suspended, and braking was accomplished through hydraulic disk brakes. Each door extended high into the roof for greater ease of entry, and the frame was of the "step-down" variety— at a time when many domestic cars required that passengers step up to climb in.

The question asked of me most often is, "What did Tucker do with all the money he raised to produce the car?" All I can say is that we spent $28 million on the Tucker enterprise. To fully launch the car, we would have needed a total of $50 million. A loan from the Reconstruction Finance Corporation would have made up the difference and one good word from the S.E.C. and we might have had it.

I believed at the time, as I continue to believe, that no Detroit manufacturer could have done any better with $28 million. History has proved me right, in a way, for in 1957 a similar venture exploded on the automotive horizon with a monetary force that could have brought five separate Tucker Corporations into being. Both the Tucker and its latter-day "cousin" were failures, but for completely different reasons. And one of their most obvious differences was conceptual: the Tucker was ahead of the times; the other car was barely keeping up!

Preston's twenty-year-old daughter, Marilyn, christened the very first Tucker car (right)—and unwittingly showered her father with champagne, much to her mother's delight. When the car was shipped to Washington, D.C., for a special show (see invitation reproduced below), it drew crowds outside a capital hotel (below right). Preston himself is shown behind the wheel.

You are cordially invited to attend

an exclusive and private preview

of America's first completely new car in fifty years

the **Tucker '48**

Presidential Ballroom, Hotel Statler, Washington, D. C.

Monday the seventh of July

from eleven A. M. until ten P. M.

Preston Thomas Tucker

This is the excitingly different automobile produced in the former B-29 Engine Plant in Chicago, the world's largest factory of its type.

We sincerely hope you can attend in order to see for yourself what can be accomplished for the public, for thousands of new automotive dealer opportunities and for national employment through proper adaptation of a war surplus property. We are convinced our automobile is an outstanding example of progress achieved through the American system of free enterprise.

Please present this invitation for the admittance
of you and your party

Tucker Number Two
THE CARIOCA

by ALEXIS DE SAKHNOFFSKY

In 1955, six years after his acquittal by a federal court, the late Preston Tucker was back in the news once more. Although his initial dream of creating an auto-building enterprise had been crushed, he announced that he was planning to develop and build a new Tucker car, which like its predecessor, would render all other road cars obsolete. It would be a utility car that performed like a sports car, and would be geared to sell for less than the lowest priced stock car then on the market. Alexis de Sakhnoffsky, who designed the car, wrote this article shortly before his death last year. Although the Tucker-de Sakhnoffsky combine produced a novel concept, Tucker was unable to obtain financing, and the project died with him.

Preston Tucker was easy to know and hard not to like. In the four years prior to his death of lung cancer, our acquaintance, which began strictly on a business level, grew into a close friendship. And I came to admire his unvarying optimism and consistently logical approach to the most complex problems. How can I describe such a man as Tucker? "Audacious" is the word that comes quickest to mind, for it was indeed audacious of him, in the first place, to have tried to invade a field dominated by experienced industrial giants. Then, though he suffered a moral as well as monetary defeat in the downfall of his enterprise, he began immediately to conceive of means to try again.

Hounded by creditors, his own credit at its lowest ebb, and bitter at the manifest injustices that had been dealt him, Preston racked his brain to find another approach to the problem of turning his dream of a car into a reality. He came to me to seek help in putting down on paper what he planned as the Tucker Number Two.

Preston felt that much of the sheer enjoyment of motoring was missed when you drove a boxy family sedan, functional though it may be. He wanted to build cars that were fun to drive. His conception of a fun car was a sporty looking vehicle of intriguing design, whose performance was sparkling, and which could be sold at a profit for $1,000.

My first meeting with him took place in 1952 in his Ypsilanti, Michigan, headquarters where he had salvaged a rather well-equipped machine shop from his first automotive venture. There, laid out on long tables, was a complete assortment of automotive parts that could be purchased readily on a C.O.D. basis. Noting my surprise, Preston explained that as soon as a new model produced by any of the Big Three automakers reached the manufacturing stage, the "gray market" immediately tooled up to produce identical or facsimile parts for the replacement business. Such facsimile parts included wheels, steering mechanisms, electrical systems, transmissions, radiator cores, brakes and what have you. Some of them were already in sub-assembly form.

The designer's problem had thus been simplified, or made more complex, depending on how you looked at it: he would have to create a car that utilized a maximum number of available parts and a minimum number of parts that had to be built from new tooling. Also, it should be a car that could be put together with little difficulty. Aware of the pitfalls, but fascinated by the thought of becoming associated with such an incredibly imaginative man as Preston Tucker, I agreed to submit ideas for the design of the Tucker Number Two.

In his original car building program, Preston had employed a team of bright, young engineers who had helped him develop the first Tucker car. Later, unable to remain idle, these men drifted away, accepting jobs with various established manufacturers. It is a tribute to Preston's magnetism that all these men remained on call in the event he would ever be able to start up again. The loyalty of some of the men I met personally was heartwarming.

Preston's ideas were unorthodox, to say the least, and he was unabashedly dogmatic about imposing them. For one thing, he claimed that research had proved that from ten to twelve pounds of accumulated mud, gravel and tar are carried at times under each of the four fenders of a conventionally designed car. His solution: cycle fenders, which could be removed easily for cleaning and thereby abet the road performance of the car. He also insisted on what I can only describe as Pierce-Arrow-like headlights, rising part-way out of the front fenders, which would turn with the wheels as the car was steered. And of course there would be a third headlight—in the center, and stationary —because it had now become a sort of Tucker trademark.

The third Tucker mandate was a rear engine. Preston believed that this location offered several advantages. There would be much less noise; the front end could have a slim and streamlined shape; and there would be added safety for passengers in case of a front-end collision.

The instrument panel of the new car was to be the acme of simplicity: an oversized speedometer surrounded by four blinkers—for fuel, oil, temperature and amperes. The pointed tail of the eventual design had been advised by the racing car designer Harry Miller, with whom Preston had worked earlier in his career and whom Preston deeply respected. In fact, one of Miller's sketches was turned over to me for inspiration. To further the fun car notion, there was to be an unusual, curved rear-seat design, reminiscent of that of a motorboat.

The greatest deterrent to producing the car was the cost of body and sheet-metal dies. Naturally, some die work (hood and rear-engine cover, specifically) had to be considered. But for constructing doors and other components involving simple one-way stretch or rolled operations, Preston received an enthusiastic response from a number of house-trailer builders. He believed, and I concurred, that since composite bodies had given more than satisfactory service to trailer owners for many years, there was no reason why such assemblies could not be used on the new Tucker car and shipped directly to the buyer along with the rest of the parts. The Tucker fun car was to be sold in kit form.

Since Preston's credit was nil, a Detroit bank was designated to act as a kind of trustee and deal directly with the parts manufacturers. When a customer made a suitable and sufficient payment to the bank— either directly or through a finance company—orders were to be immediately dispatched by the bank to participating manufacturers, who in turn began shipping parts to the customer. Bills of lading were also to be credited by the fiduciary bank to each manufacturer, but no bill was actually to be paid until all the parts had been delivered.

Tucker knew that among the nation's repair garage owners there were a great many who were eager to obtain Big Three franchises, but unable to, for one reason or another. Preston hoped to tap this reservoir of frustrated car dealers and also to provide the future Tucker owner with a service outlet. The customer would be urged to have his car assembled by a specially authorized garage owner for a prearranged fee of $60 (that is, ten hours at $6 an hour, as outlined in a manual accompanying the components). In this manner, the new Tucker company would acquire a dealer organization, and the customer would be assured of service for his car.

Hearing about plans to build this car, Juscelino Kubitschek, who was then the president of Brazil and a friend of Preston's, offered inducements in the form of tax-free plants, if the car could be assembled in his country. Intrigued by the offer, Tucker made several trips to Brazil and even considered launching the car in South America. Because of this possibility, Preston and I agreed to call the car the Tucker Carioca—Carioca being the name of the ballroom version of the samba and also the name applied to a citizen of Rio de Janeiro.

Although I did not agree entirely with Preston's conception of how the car should look, I prepared a number of roughs that embodied his ideas, and from these he selected the design herewith. Close scrutiny of the concept will reveal some flaws, of course, but it is reasonable to assume that many of the inherent problems would have been solved eventually. Unfortunately, the project progressed no farther than the rough-sketch stage, which was a profound disappointment to me, for the idea of a strictly fun car is always present in the auto designer's mind. And I think this would have been a fun car to build. ✥

the Knight

FROM THE MONTAGU MOTOR MUSEUM,
BEAULIEU, ENGLAND

the Bloodless Revolution—such was the bold phrase by which Sir David Salomons, mayor of Tunbridge Wells, England, in 1895, described the approaching replacement of the horse. Parliament had not that confidence, however, for road legislation had long since placed motor vehicles on a par with the traction engine, thus providing an effective damper on British motor experimenters. Not all were dissuaded, of course. John Henry Knight of Farnham, builder of a steam carriage in 1868 and inventor of the Trusty Oil Engine, was one who was not. In 1895 he built what is believed to be the first British gasoline car to be operated on the road. Originally it was a three-wheeled vehicle weighing 1,075 pounds and developing nearly one horsepower at 500 revolutions. With one passenger, a speed of eight miles per hour was possible on level road; another passenger slowed it down a bit. So silent running was the vehicle that horses reportedly took no notice of it. The *law* did, however. One fall day while driving through Farnham, Knight was arrested. He had no traction-engine license, and his vehicle was not preceded by a man armed with a red flag—a regulation no longer required though still enforced. This brush with the law did not deter Knight. He experimented still. For stability he added another wheel to his vehicle, and demonstrated it at London's Crystal Palace Motor Exhibition in May of 1896. Its horizontal water-cooled engine drove a counter-shaft by two belts for fast and slow speeds. Front wheels were carried in bicycle forks sprung by coil springs, in quasi i.f.s. style. No arrangement for reversing was used or thought necessary. Knight never marketed his car. Its purpose was primarily political: to rouse public opinion against the inane restrictions hampering the use of motor carriages in England. It was a purpose fulfilled. Knight's car and his arrest were among the factors responsible for the more liberal road legislation passed in November 1896.   *R. L. Perrin*

71

A dutch treat

THE NATIONAL AUTOMOBILE MUSEUM IN HOLLAND

photography by TOM BURNSIDE

Here's a Dutch Treat that's a feast for just a gulden. The place is Driebergen, Holland, and the treat is the Nationaal Museum Van de Automobiel.

Driebergen, a city whose history dates back to the Fourteenth Century, lies about an hour's drive southeast of Amsterdam. Encircled by meadow and forest, it is primarily a residential area with all the charm and peace one associates with Holland—the old mansions, the medieval town hall and, of course, the gardens.

The museum lies adjacent to and is an important part of the Instituut voor de Autohandel, Holland's oldest technical and commercial college for the automotive trade. Both museum and college are guided by the indefatigable spirit of Alec Riemer, a remarkably young man despite his seventy-five years.

In opening the museum in August of 1953, Mr. Riemer successfully put his cart before the horse. One large hall had been built, and the assistance of two Dutch automobile clubs had been enlisted to provide the exhibits. Shortly before the museum doors were to be thrown open, however, Mr. Riemer discovered there were too few cars to spread around too much floor. The extra space was filled in on opening day with an oil prospecting display lent by the Shell Oil Company, a display returned the following year as more antique cars made their way to Driebergen. The museum has been expanding ever since. Within seven years its area was doubled, and today there are three halls displaying automobiles, a 220-seat theater-lecture hall in which films about the pioneer days of motoring are shown several times a day and a congenial coffeeshop.

Congeniality, indeed, sets the tone for the entire museum. English-speaking guides are available to ease any language difficulty, and visitors are welcome to take as many photographs as their film will permit. Over a hundred thousand visitors pass through the museum gates annually, bringing in enough cash to make the collection self-supporting, if, as Mr. Riemer says, "we are a little 'easy' about booking all costs."

Of the forty cars currently displayed, about two-thirds are in running condition, and they

Between the years 1899 and 1925, the Dutch Automobile Works produced the Spyker automobile. The two-seater, two-cylinder model above was built in 1906 and raced with scant success against British cycle cars. The earlier four-cylinder version of this model was better known. The Panhard-Levassor at right was built in 1912. Panhard, one of the oldest automotive firms still in production, was among the first to fit engines in the front of their cars. This beautifully bodied coupé de ville with brass lamps and radiator expresses Emile Levassor's belief, "If you build heavy, you build strong."

all take repeated trips to the college workshop for an "all-over," as Mr. Riemer says, to keep them in top condition. The Spyker, Holland's best-known pioneer motorcar, is represented by four models, notably the one pictured on the preceding page. That is the famous 1902 race model boasting such automotive firsts as six cylinders, four-wheel drive and transmission-based front wheel brakes. Other noteworthy cars on display range from an early F.N. and an 1894 Benz hunting car to a 1912 German Cyclonette with front wheel drive and a 1930 sixteen-cylinder Marmon cabriolet.

Mr. Riemer attributes the success of his museum in part to the fact that it is more than a gathering place for antique car exhibits. It is also a showplace, dressed with the world's largest collection of registration plates, automobile prints, engravings, and posters like the Georges-Richard poster pictured on the preceding page. There is a fascinating display of old motors, many of them cutaways to show, for example, a valveless or sleeve-valve powerplant. A good many electrically driven motors are to be seen, as well as hot-air motors, a Diesel engine, a 1926 eight-in-line Studebaker and a pre-1930 Cadillac V-8 all-aluminum engine. Of interest, too, is a forerunner of the Wankel motor constructed by a Dutchman in 1929. Other displays feature gearboxes, lamps and tires—one of the latter a tubeless model from 1894. And, scattered throughout the museum are mannequins—motorists and their ladies—dressed for driving in the pioneer automobile era.

Humor and automobiliana frequently go hand in hand, and a visit to the national auto museum in Holland would not be complete without a glimpse of the everyday gadgets shaped like automobiles that began appearing soon after the horseless carriage was accepted as a reality. One can scarcely envision the utility of a teapot in the form of a motor vehicle, but in the early 1900's it was available for those who wanted to try. More practical, perhaps, was the box for salt, pepper and mustard decorated with a "road

Built at the Grégoire works at Poissy, the 1907 Grégoire traveling coach, above, has four cylinders and four-fold hydraulic shock absorbers. A practical feature for that day was the brass disk on the front window which could be removed when the window was frozen, leaving a peep hole through which the driver might follow the road. The interior includes a woodwork gate behind which parcels could be stored. An interesting hybrid is the 1900 Brasier at right with its contrastive rear sprung wheels. Inside its massive hood is a two-cylinder motor and a radiator manufactured by de Dion, Bouton et Cie.

hog"—a swine complete with goggles—sitting smugly at the steering wheel. For the musically inclined pioneer motorist there was a cigarette box with cigars or cigarettes stored under the car seat. To get to the contents, the seat had to be lifted, whereupon the smoker was greeted with strains from the opera *Der Freischütz*.

The contents of the museum alone are enough to hold the attention of any visitor for at least a full day, but a further inducement to linger in its halls is Mr. Riemer himself. His anecdotes of early motoring days are legion, and his enthusiasm for the world of the automobile is contagious. He recalls vividly that day in 1898 when the Paris-Amsterdam-Paris tour passed through his native town of Arnhem, and he ran away from school to see the cars, smell the automobile fumes and taste the dust. His schoolmaster, he relates, was sadly unaware of the historical value of the event. But young Alec had, perhaps, an instinctive regard for the automobile's future. As a lad of ten he would frequently ride in the rear of the "coach and four" his father drove and manipulate a walking stick and umbrella in imitation of gear changing and using the handbrake.

Family plans for his future were channeled into the business of jobbing horses out to the nobility, and at the age of eighteen he was manager of a company that owned several stables in the Hague. But an era was ending, and because so many people in England were replacing their horses and carriages with a motorcar, the value of a single brougham—even from the famed John Barker—plummeted; rarely would it fetch more than five pounds when sold at auction. Alec Riemer decided very quickly to become part of the new era as an importer of English motor vehicles in Holland.

Much has been written about the hazards of being an automobile dealer during the first twenty-five years of the industry's growth. Alec Riemer learned the hard way "how not to do it." He wanted to tell others, and as editor and owner of the first trade paper for the garage

The 1907 Spyker above sold for approximately $2,400. It was advertised as "no oil-no dust," the latter being realized by a metal pan underneath the entire chassis, a feature of many contemporary automobiles. Over 2,300 Benz cars were built between 1885 and 1901. The best known of the Benz models and the first car in the world to be manufactured in quantity was the Benz-Velo. The 1894 model at right features a one-cylinder horizontal engine, full elliptical springing between front axle and steering mechanism, an open crankshaft and flywheel, and surface carburetor. Top speed was about 10 mph.

business in Holland, he began. Although the paper was soon taken over by the dealers' organization, Riemer remained in charge as editor. The basic problems of automotive dealers remained too; with inadequate guidance from manufacturers, their livelihood was haphazard at best. Mr. Riemer realized that conditions would not improve until young people entering the field could get proper training, both technically and commercially. That in mind, he started an experimental one-year course in September, 1930, with four young students. It proved to be a measurable success. With the occupation of Holland in 1944, the German High Command wanted to conscript all the school's students for work in Germany. This was prevented when Mr. Riemer closed the school, hid the records and sent his eighty-six students home quickly. At the war's end, the school was reopened. Today approximately five hundred students from sixteen to twenty-two years of age attend, and future plans call for the establishment of courses in English to attract more international students.

As principal of the Instituut voor de Autohandel, Mr. Riemer is justly proud that his graduates now work in fifty-eight different countries. "My boys" is the way Riemer always refers to the school's students. And it was for them that he made plans thirteen years ago to open an automobile museum. He was influenced, of course, by the fact that there was no similar museum in Holland, but his guiding impetus was to create a place to attract young people who love motorcars and to encourage his boys to develop respect for and knowledge about antique cars. Today the museum's cars are tended in the college workshops, and many students serve as museum guides in summer months.

That the Nationaal Museum Van de Automobiel has become a favorite stopping place for international visitors is another fact of which its director may be justly proud. It verifies Mr. Riemer's contention that "Holland is more than Amsterdam."

—Cullen Thomas

IN THE ITALIAN STYLE

by GIANNI ROGLIATTI

PININFARINA *abarth 1000*

Presented here are five distinctive new cars from the style-setting
Italian *carrozzerias*—a pacesetting look down the road ahead. To add
sophistication to a popular car idea, Pininfarina designed the Abarth
at right on a chassis that had derived from the Fiat 850. It is fitted
with a rear-mounted, four-cylinder, 982 cc engine that provides a top
speed of over 100 mph. The high back end, well-raked windshield and
sloped, slim front section blend in aerodynamic harmony. The surgically
clean body is embellished with but a single line: thin-strip suggestions
of bumpers meeting a fold or "dihedron" on the sides. Inside, three-piece
construction of the seats allows passenger and driver to mold themselves
into position, and the diagonally pleated leather cleverly secures occupants
against lateral and vertical movements. A light ogival fairing for
instruments takes the place of the traditional automobile dashboard.

photography by Giorgio Bellia

MICHELOTTI osi 850 berlinetta

This berlinetta, OSI's production prototype, was begun with a Fiat 850 platform, a popular choice for European coachbuilders because of its size, maneuverability and economy. The engine was mildly souped up by SIATA, raising maximum speed from 78 mph to the 90 mph range—quite sufficient for cruising on the Autostrada without getting bored. Giovanni Michelotti designed the OSI body ten inches lower than the Fiat standard; this provides a good aerodynamic coefficient,

an important factor to Michelotti who designs all his models in one-tenth scale and wind tunnel tests them in Turin. The front of the car is built around rectangular Cibiè headlights and houses the trunk and spare tire. The lines flow back to a concave-shaped tail, which looks over the backlight clusters and mates to the sides by a crease resembling the stroke of a sculptor's chisel. The chromed grille provides air intake for the engine and cooling, and a swivel of the license plate reveals the fuel tank cap.

BERTONE *alfa romeo canguro*

Creating something different and yet practical on a chassis like the Alfa Romeo Giulia *tubolare* was a formidable assignment. But it was from the *tubolare*—the Alfa racing model used in grand touring competition—that Bertone designed his Canguro. Answering his desire for a lower car, the Canguro rises just forty inches from the ground. For a more streamlined appearance, the biggest double-curved windshield and rear window ever made for a car was designed. All known weight-saving tricks were used to ascertain that the Canguro would not outweigh the standard racing type, and some exquisite artwork was employed to fashion a single-piece trussed engine hood. Both weight-saving and aesthetic was the use of an aeronautical industry cement to fasten the window glass panels to their metal frames. A clever ruse are the four-leaf clovers on both sides of the car; they disguise ventilation openings. The Canguro, which in Italian means "kangaroo," is available from Bertone.

PININFARINA *fiat 2300 s*

The familiar lines and the subtle changing of Pininfarina's style are evident in this elegant coupé. There is the well-known curve of the roof that seems cantilevered from the rear, and the near absence of chrome except for bumpers and a running strip under the doors. Gone, however, is the squarish flat grille front; replacing it is a more penetrating aerodynamic form with headlights streamlined by glass fairings and the air intake beneath the bumper. What were the fins of yesterday are now simple edges to mark the rear fender line. The rear deck is flat and uncluttered. The elegant exterior is matched inside the car with anatomic wrap-around front seats of white leather and a noise-abating, reflection-guarding instrument panel of expanded resin with ample padding. The steering wheel is wood rimmed with aluminum sheet spokes.

GHIA *renault r-8 sports coupé*

A car with a definite personality—bold and different, yet pleasing and practical—was the order that Ghia manager Dr. Giacomo Gaspardo-Moro gave his designers. Their work reflects both the old and the new; the rounded, very French lines hearken back to the prewar coachwork of Saoutchik and Figoni et Falaschi for Talbots, Bugattis and Delahayes, yet the front section is inherently Renault. A car designed around the two people who are carried inside, this Ghia prototype provides comfortable seating, excellent visibility and ample luggage space. Its estimated top speed is 120 mph, the result of a Gordini engine modification and the lower drag of the body. Although imposing in appearance, the car is small, with a wheelbase three inches shorter than the standard R8. It was designed to have a wide market appeal.

COLIN CHAPMAN
builder of champions by stephen f. wilder

In eighteen years of enterprise as the builder of Lotus cars, Colin Chapman has brought precision engineering and aerodynamic subtlety to the racing of automobiles, a mechanically oriented sport that has lingered long and lazily under the blacksmith's spreading chestnut tree. What is surprising, in this age of scientific surfeit, is that nobody did it sooner.

No mere innovator, the thirty-seven-year-old Englishman has been eminently successful at his game and is generally considered the foremost racing car designer extant. Since 1947, when the first squared-off, super-simple Lotus appeared—visually it seemed a smithy's version of a Rolls-Royce roadster in miniature—Chapman's cars have won more races throughout the world than has any other marque, including Bugatti and Ferrari.

Colin Chapman's interest in automobiles and his involvement in the auto sport dates from his days as an engineering student at London University. For more than a year, then, he turned a handsome profit in a second-hand car business. With the postwar revival of petrol rationing, the business collapsed, and he was left with an unwanted inventory. One of the leftovers was a 1930 Austin 7 saloon, which with the tools he had and the technical assistance he acquired, he converted into a "special" to compete in Trials events.

In England's sports lexicon, Trials are low-speed, low-budget substitutes for auto racing, and they are not held on ovals or circuits, but on wintry hillsides. The cars run up, one at a time, and the point of the contest is to get as near the top of each marked-out section as you can. Notable characteristics of these Trials are the ingenious designs of the cars, the equally ingenious rules, the earnestly helpful passengers who bounce up and down furiously in an effort to improve the rear tires' bite, and the omnipresence of mud. British winters are as wet as they are long.

From assailing muddy English slopes, Colin Chapman progressed to racing wheel to wheel on abandoned R.A.F. airfields. The Trials had given him an insuperable obsession for racing;

it was no longer just a schoolboy's pastime. He graduated from the university in mid-1948 with a degree in structural engineering. The following October he was called into the R.A.F. to begin flight training. His time was not his own for the next twelve months, but he spent his furloughs in a frenzy of work on a second Trials car. Back in mufti, he accelerated his car-building activities, even though he took a job first with a structural steel concern, then with the British Aluminum Company, each on a full-time basis.

With a background in engineering and experience in aeronautics, he was beginning his career as a racing car designer with several advantages. He was well schooled in problems relating to stress and support of the mass, and he understood drag, thrust and wind resistance. In addition, he was aware that cars are basically load-bearing structures, just like buildings and bridges, and the airplanes he had flown.

Equally useful to Chapman—as it always has been—was his innate ability to penetrate a problem right to the core, without fumbling

THE LOTUS MARK 1

THE LOTUS MARK 6

with peripheral details. Thus the brilliance of a Chapman design is in its directness. It seems so simple that in assessing its innovations, you wonder why they had not been thought of before. In some instances they had been, but probably had not been fully realized in execution, or perhaps had been buried in otherwise inferior cars. In auto racing, as in other fields, the flattery of imitation is usually reserved for winners. A part of Chapman's genius is his ability to recognize a jewel of an idea in a flawed setting.

Speaking of flaws, Chapman has consistently worked under what can be a crippling handicap for a racing car designer: he buys his engines instead of building them. Lotuses thus have had to win on the strength of their light weight and agility—for which Chapman and his organization were directly responsible—since at least one competitor has always had equal power and others often have had more. As Chapman was to find, the most powerful engines are not always for sale.

Using engines whose capacities for winning were uncertain, Chapman has had to produce his champions from a blend of elements whose selection and refinement have more than made up for whatever lack of power there has been. Chapman has successfully brought to racing a number of engineering advances plus a variety of novel suspension geometries that defy brief description but account largely for the Lotus's roadholding and maneuverability. In addition, he has built aerodynamic bodies that are tested by cotton tuft instead of by eyeball.

Colin Chapman knows well that an auto designer is not necessarily a man in a smock hunched over a drawing table or a man with a slide rule carrying blueprints under his arm. He can be either of these, of course. He can also be a man who arranges other people's ideas and schemes—and in so doing, conceives what appears to be something distinctive and totally new. This, in part, is Colin Chapman. As a designer of racing cars, he selects components, often from a catalogue, and rarely designs more than the fiber glass or metal units that will bind the components and the driver together. He

does not work alone in this endeavor. He has always had highly skilled associates working with him, and in recent years, his cars have been produced by whole teams of engineers and designers.

If Chapman had grown up in Los Angeles, instead of in London, his cars would have been called "hot rods" instead of "specials." As a matter of fact, he rather resented having his first brainchild referred to as just another Austin Special, even though it was essentially just that. So he christened it Lotus, later suffixing Mark 1 when he started on his second car. Every car Chapman has built since then carries that name, but he apparently plans to carry its meaning to his grave. It has been suggested that Chapman spent so much time thinking about his first car, when he should have been concerned with school work, that his teachers regarded him a lotus-eater because he daydreamed in class. No one could have guessed that Chapman's daydreaming would lay the cornerstone for a startlingly successful career.

On January 1, 1952, less than four years out

of college, Chapman established the Lotus Engineering Company. A full-time nucleus was hired, but Chapman could not devote all his energies to the firm for three more years. He would come to the plant at eight in the morning, spend an hour and a half there and then hasten to his "real" job by nine-thirty. He would be back at Lotus by 6 p.m. and work until two or three in the morning. It was a rigorous schedule that left him little time to sleep, much less catch his breath, but it allowed him to sustain two full-time professions.

Early in his career, Chapman worked mostly with standard components—mass produced items of high reliability and low cost. The first few Lotuses were built on modified Austin frames; only the bodies and the arrangement of components were really new. But with the Mark 6, first produced in 1953, Chapman began building Lotuses in which even the frames—the cars' structural backbones—were original. The Mark 6, built for sale as well as competition, was produced in kit form for the buyer to put together. This feature provided great sales attrac-

tion because it circumvented the sales tax; it was also a boon to Lotus, which did not yet have adequate assembly facilities.

As Chapman prospered, he designed and built racing cars in which more and more parts were created from raw stock. He also turned gradually from the comparatively humble fields of club-level sports car racing to the international arena of single-seater road racing. The latter is usually called Grand Prix racing; though the prizes are no longer so grand, the fame continues to be.

Chapman entered these lists in 1957, his tenth year of building cars, and by 1959 he was fielding a car that was easily the sleekest and technically the most impressive of its contemporaries, the Lotus 16. Front-engined, it had the best power-to-weight ratio (for acceleration), the smallest frontal area (for maximum speed) and a suspension that experts considered the most advanced of its time. Unfortunately, the 16's were so complicated they often broke down, and even those that stayed together couldn't go fast enough to win. Not even once.

Having come so far, and having failed so thoroughly and conspicuously, Chapman had good reason to ponder the future. He felt confident that he was smarter than any other designer, but that knowledge was small consolation when he was being beaten time after time by cars that he felt were inferior.

Aware that mechanical unreliability was only part of his problem, Chapman gave especial thought to his self-established precept of handling—that above all else, a car must be completely stable in any turn or bend, right up to the maximum speed at which it could be taken. In contrast, the car that was beating him, the rear-engined Cooper, which had an identical powerplant, proceeded around corners with great dispatch and very little dignity. Sometimes it looked very tidy; other times its rear end appeared to be "hung out" in a precarious fashion. By contrast, Lotuses hardly ever spun or seemed out of control, even when they were. Chapman concluded that he had been deceiving himself, for he knew that a hard-driven Cooper rarely went off the road,

91

although it might get sideways for a time. Chapman decided, on the evidence, that it was worth forfeiting a modicum of stability to obtain an increase in controllability.

It must be stressed, at this point, that tires do not lose their grip—in the sense of letting go—when a driver exceeds his cornering speed limit. They merely cease *increasing* their grip. A car skidding sideways, for example, will come to a stop in about the same distance as if its brakes were locked and it were headed forward. The Lotuses of the late Fifties were certainly stable, but this was not always an asset. When the adhesion limit of their tires was reached, the front wheels were often the first to be affected. They thus became unsteerable, allowing, if not impelling, the car to go off the road in a uselessly "stable" nose-first manner.

Another useless facet of Chapman's design was apparent in the 16. The drive shaft of this rear-drive car took a circuitous path to the rear axle, so that the driver could sit lower—thus reducing frontal area and increasing top speed. The 16's drive shaft therefore incorporated four universal joints. These produced a considerable dissipation of power, as did the tilted installation of the engine. The result was *less* speed instead of more.

The complexity of the 16 had not been a sudden aberration. As far back as the Mark 8 of 1954, Chapman had made a truss frame so thoroughly triangulated that it took twenty-four man-hours to remove the engine and more than twelve to replace it!

After a careful evaluation, in the fall of 1959, Chapman revised several of his precepts. He resolved that future Lotuses would emphasize simplicity and give the edge to controllability over directional stability. Moving the engine from front to rear was the most logical way to get rid of the four burdensome joints, and as a fringe benefit, the entire drive shaft. Chapman's first rear-engined car was the 18.

It must be stressed that the desired tail-hanging-out kind of cornering behavior, which had been typical of the tail-heavy Cooper, was achieved in the 18's *suspension*—not, as is commonly thought, by moving its engine to the rear. In fact, the Lotus 18 had four per cent *less* weight on the rear wheels than had its front-engined predecessor of the same weight. In a sense, by the way, both the 16 and the 18 were mid-engined cars. The 16, with its engine well back from the front wheels, was just about as tail-heavy as the Coopers it was losing to.

The 18 was long in conception but quickly produced. Five weeks off the drawing boards, the first car was being raced. As Chapman had hoped, it combined the twin virtues of simplicity and sturdiness to arrive at the desired goal: the ability to win. The 18 was the first Lotus to win a major Grand Prix (Stirling Moss at Monaco, 1960), and every Lotus single-seater that followed it has been clearly derived from it, albeit much sleeker. With one of these successors, the 25, Lotus won the FIA's World Championship for Racing Car Constructors in 1963.

Every new Lotus design is given a number, as are redesigns, if the cars are visibly altered. The designs are numbered consecutively, but there are some gaps, for not every Lotus design

THE LOTUS 29 THE LOTUS 30

has touched tires to the ground. The Mark 5 was reserved for a project that fell by the wayside, and 13 was eschewed for the sound business reason that racing drivers are notoriously superstitious, even if Chapman himself is not. The latest Lotus, at this writing, is the 38, this year's Indianapolis car, Ford-powered as were the preceding Lotus 29 and 34. The 37, or Three-Seven as the hucksters have it, is an updated version, with independent suspension, of the popular stark Seven, itself a lengthily gestated revision of the Mark 6.

Yet to be announced is a car to employ Coventry Climax's flat 16. Supporting it in Formula One events will be the new 33B, a slight revision of last year's 33. For competition in other European formulas, Chapman has distilled the experience gained from building the 27 and 32, and come up with the 35, a road racer designed to accept and race with four-cylinder engines that vary all the way from 1000 to 2500 cc!

From the foregoing, it can be seen that the annual model change is not peculiar to Detroit. However, in contrast to the numerical as well as mechanical changes made in Lotus racing cars, Chapman has been building high-performance road cars for the past several years, and these continue with little change.

Serious students of auto design recognize that racing cars share precious few similarities with passenger cars other than their mutual use of four wheels and an engine. Most also recognize that any car can be raced, although not necessarily with success. What few appreciate is that because the racing car's purpose is simpler to define—to win a race within a given framework of rules—its design statement is also simpler. Success in the esoteric field of speed and performance may require knowledge of certain "secrets" that are gained only with racing experience. But given this knowledge and a powerplant that is at least the equal of the competition's, it is far simpler to design a car that needs no provision for passengers, luggage or a heater-defroster, and very little concern for comfort, weatherproofing, or ease of entry and egress. (In some racing cars, the steering wheel has to be removed to permit the driver to climb in and out!) Another advantage is that the racing car need not be designed to suit existent tooling.

Although passenger cars may be more complex, racing cars do constitute a singular challenge. When a racing car comes to the line, its designer's capabilities and limitations are immediately thrust on display. His reputation can be made by one extraordinary racing performance—even if the driver deserves the credit—and destroyed by the smallest misjudgment.

Little more than guts, talent and imagination are required to enter the racing field. Without them the threshold is an impenetrable barrier. The situation in the passenger car field, particularly since the end of World War II, has been vastly different. Nowadays, mass production requires mass merchandising; men like Preston Tucker and Henry J. Kaiser took on more than they bargained for when they plunged headlong into the passenger car business. Both men went out of business, their enterprises nipped in the bud. Conversely, Chapman's Lotus business has blossomed. Why? One reason is

THE LOTUS 33

THE LOTUS 34

that he is enormously talented; another is that whereas they plunged, he *eased* himself into the passenger car business. Despite their abundance of guts and imagination, neither could cope successfully with the exhausting requisites of mass distribution.

However accidentally, Chapman followed a more circumspect, and hindsight shows, an extremely logical path. In 1957, with nearly ten years of racing car design behind him, he built a sports car that he hoped would combine the high-speed potential and maneuverability of a racing car with those aspects of comfort, efficiency and good handling that are desired in a vehicle for the public roads. He named this car the Lotus Elite; numerically it's the 14.

Conceived as a GT car—to compete with, say, the Porsche 356—it is a sleek two-seater coupé with an integral body/frame of fiber-glass-reinforced plastic. The car was technically a designer's tour de force. And though it looked and went very fast indeed, riding in it was as noisy as being sealed inside a tympany. The closed body shell mercilessly amplified the vibrations

of the detuned Coventry Climax engine and the chassis-mounted differential casing, the latter an essential element of independent rear suspension.

Despite its startling newness, the Elite was imperfect. And though many of its attributes were attractive, this first Lotus for the road proved a wallflower in the salesroom. Undismayed, Chapman raced the car successfully in the burgeoning GT category. It was clear to all who knew him, however, that Colin Chapman had ambitions beyond the desire to collect laurel wreaths and silver trophies.

In 1963 he produced a second effort in the field of non-racing vehicles. The car, which he called the Lotus Elan, is a study in similarities to and contrasts with its predecessor; happily it represents the best of both comparisons. The differences constitute lessons learned, and the number of changes is a measure of the complexity of designing cars for general use and of Chapman's ability to apply the knowledge gleaned from his mistakes.

Like the Elite, the Elan is a tiny two-seater with fiber glass body, four-speed transmission

and four-wheel independent suspension. Each car has its engine in the front. Whereas the Elite was produced prior to Chapman's rear-engine period, the Elan is the first front-engined Lotus since the ill-fated 16.

The Elan is not a throwback, however. Its engine is up front because Chapman and his staff agreed that the forward location was best for the car. The Volkswagen and Corvair offer tangible proof that in a rear-engined car, after space has been provided to allow the front wheels to turn and front-seat riders to stretch their legs, there is almost no room for luggage. In the Elan, the engine and drive train form a narrow central unit, with ample foot- and legroom to either side. Luggage can be stashed in the full-width space between the non-steering rear wheels.

Closely related to the problem of where to place the engine is the need to select the most efficient frame construction and layout. In his latest single-seater racing cars, Chapman has wrapped the driver in a semi-monocoque tube that integrates the fuel tanks with the stream-

THE CLEANNESS OF THE ELAN CHASSIS IS MATCHED BY THE NO-NONSENSE LOOK OF ITS INSTRUMENT PANEL. AT LEFT IS ONE OF THE ELAN'S RETRACTABLE HEADLIGHTS.

lined body. The outer skin in the cockpit area of these cars contains fuel on one side, slices air on the other and carries all frame loads.

In designing the Elan, Chapman went a step farther. Although he was building a two-passenger car, he began with what was essentially a single-seater's body/frame, squaring its sides and omitting the customary cockpit opening. He then placed the two seats on either side of the resulting box that encloses the drive shaft. Beyond the cockpit, the Elan's frame widens into a fork at each end, providing easy engine accessibility and improving the means for receiving loads from front and rear suspensions.

The Elan has a more severely aerodynamic shape than the Elite, and many people consider it less aesthetic. Whether you like its looks, you are struck by the simplicity of its body and by its tight, uninterrupted curves. The low, tapering front-end shape is enhanced by recessed and covered headlights; they fold out of sight in one second flat when the lights are switched off—fast enough so the lights can still be flashed when necessary.

In contrast to the Elite, which had an integral body/frame, the Elan has a separate self-supporting body that is bolted to the frame with rubber insulating pads at fourteen points as an aid to noise reduction. "An ounce of rubber is worth a volume of acoustical theory,"

claims Chapman, and he must be right, for the Elan is definitely quieter than the Elite. Another reason for this is that the Elan is a convertible (a detachable hard top is available, however), and the Elite was not. A soft top does not reflect as much sound as might be heard inside a closed car.

Like all good sports cars, the Lotus Elan is certain to be raced by many of its owners. And they won't find it wanting. After studying the design and engineering of the car, but without actually seeing it, the SCCA's Car Classification Committee placed it in the same category (Class C) as the swiftest small sports cars, the ones that outrace Ferrari GT's and Sting Rays on the most tortuous racing circuits —and a class ahead of the already proven Elite. Those who have owned or driven the Elite and Elan are as pleased with the latter's improvement in domesticity as with its advance in dynamic performance. It represents a perfect marriage of race car and road car elements.

Despite his success as a sports and racing car builder, Colin Chapman has yet to make a serious attempt to reach the lofty and formidable passenger car preserve. The Lotus Cortina is merely a racing conversion of the mass-produced Ford Cortina sedan. You would no more call it a Lotus-built sedan than you would say that the Mustang GT-350 is built by Carroll Shelby.

But Chapman is certainly closer to being a maker of passenger cars of the four-door variety than any other "outsider" at the moment. If he happens to regard his business career as a gigantic Trials event, and there is evidence to support this, who can say how high he will climb before stopping? Take a look at the Elan's backbone frame, and you will see how easy it might be to lengthen it a couple of feet to accommodate a full back seat. A four-passenger Lotus would certainly be something to think about—especially if you were named Colin Chapman and you wanted to reach the top. ✦

95

A GRAND PRIX FOR CENTRAL PARK

By Alec Ulmann

The idea of arranging an International Grand Prix right in the heart of the greatest metropolis in the world is not a revolutionary one. It has been thought of, talked about, and even planned in detail, but each time, the project has withered under the caloric blast of the commissioner of all sacred things in New York, Mr. Robert Moses.

There can be no doubt that Central Park has the best venue of any location in the metropolitan area for a Grand Prix race, ideal both from a spectator's and a driver's point of view. The undulating roadways offer just the sort of challenging course of which racing drivers are fond and for which the present five- and six-speed GP Formula One machines are built. The many hillocks provide good spectator areas a safe distance from the course itself, yet still offering an unobstructed view of the more exciting turns of the track, and that, of course, is what the more sophisticated aficionados of motor racing like to watch.

Back in the mid-Fifties, Alexis Thompson and a few other optimistic sports car fans got so far as to interest the Police Athletic League in a Central Park Grand Prix, the proceeds of which, after expenses, were to go to that charitable organization. Several alternate circuits of two to three miles were laid out. The plan seemed logical, and the existence of cross-town lower-level cuts made possible the isolation of the course from normal park traffic. With P.A.L. being party to the arrangements, the organizers felt that crowd control and general policing would be no problem; "New York's Finest" would have gladly cooperated. Unfortunately, this project, like a few others that popped up on several occasions, fell on barren soil for the sole reason of Mr. Moses's immediate and irrevocable veto.

Robert Moses has in the last few years gained dubious national recognition as president of the New York World's Fair, a position to which he ascended in 1960 after handing down his park commission to Newbold Morris. But the twenty-six-year reign of Mr. Moses as park protector has left its mark. Although he has taken his hand out of New

York's parks, he still manages to strategically keep a finger in. Mr. Moses has always insisted that New York's Central Park is an area designed for the unhindered relaxation and recreation of the residents of the city, and that any abridgement of those rights, even for a short time and no matter for what cause, is intolerable. So it would appear that while the spirit of the former park commissioner rules over the green pastures he has dedicated to New Yorkers, chances are more than remote that no auto race will be run there.

There was a flicker of encouragement a year back when some enterprising bicycle enthusiasts secured a permit to run a six-hour bicycle race using some of the park paths. Apparently it was decided that this much milder form of road racing sport could be conducted without disturbing the grazing propensities of the population, and under those circumstances the powers that be relented. But the expected "tour de France" type enthusiasm for the event failed to materialize, and the race was totally ignored by both the press and the blasé Gothamites. So ended an event that could have started a chain reaction ushering in a more understanding climate for a Central Park Grand Prix. What embryo promoters and would-be organizers have lacked thus far is the tenacity and devotion to the sport that motivates such individuals as the president of the Monaco Automobile Club. M. Anthony Noghès devoted a decade to his efforts and did not give up until he ran the first Grand Prix de Monaco. The cars wound their way right through the main streets of Monte Carlo, a feat that no one has ever duplicated. That was in the early Twenties, and outside of the war years, the race has been repeated annually as the greatest Grand Prix of them all, bringing together the most resplendent gathering connected with motor racing, socially as well as sports-wise.

But, who knows, it might still happen here.

CENTRAL PARK CIRCUIT

*Over meadows, around baseball fields, along
ponds and lakes, the park's scenic thoroughfares merge into a splendid seven-mile circuit.*

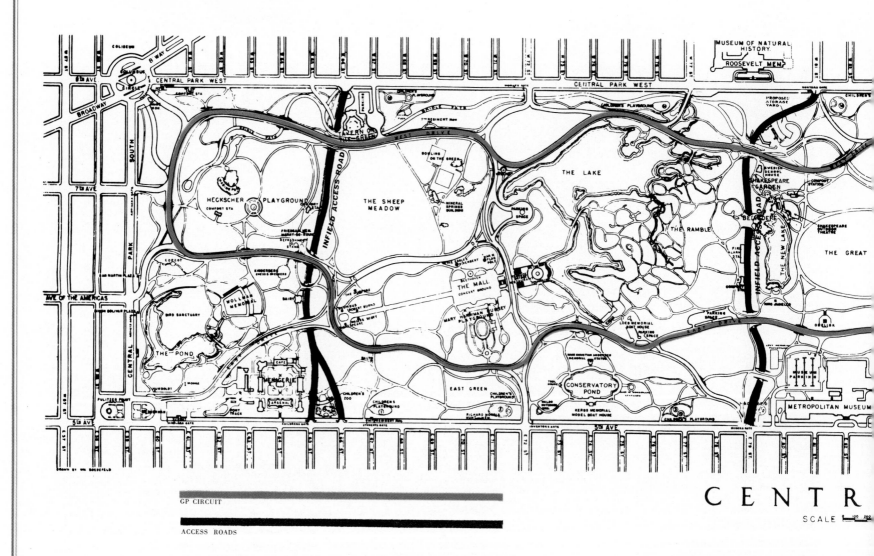

GP CIRCUIT

ACCESS ROADS

CENTR

SCALE

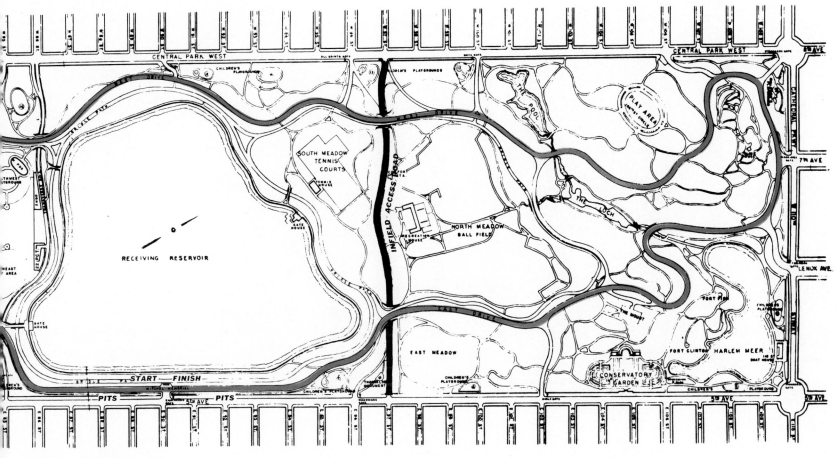

PARK

FEET

DELAUNAY
BELLEVILLE

"All things are good, dear sir. The difficulty is to choose the best. And when I say the best, I mean that which is made without fault. Do you understand me?"

The author of these words, Roger Boutet de Monvel, had no doubt that his readers *would* understand him, for he was writing specifically for men of the French aristocracy. In a preface to the catalogue of 1914-15 Delaunay-Belleville cars, Boutet de Monvel made clear the company's interest in discriminating buyers. His ornate phrases and his brother Bernard's superb watercolors, reproduced on these pages, sustain the Delaunay-Belleville image even though the car is extinct and the catalogue has yellowed from age.

"My fondest wish is that everything affecting me, my inner nature, my friends, my wardrobe and my cars—all things that are mine—could form a harmonious whole and be of good quality," Boutet de Monvel wrote. It was a nobleman's anguished cry, the essence of which was snob appeal of the highest order.

In Delaunay-Belleville's heyday, the years before World War I, the car had no peer in all of France. In appearance it was distinctive not only because of its size and ornamentation, but also because of its round radiator, which was eventually drawn into a V shape in the postwar period of the marque's decline. Copper and brass ornamentation was used extensively.

Built not so much for speed as for cruising in comfort, Delaunay-Belleville touring cars of prewar vintage largely made use of splash-lubricated engines whose side valves were inclined in relation to the cylinder axis—to provide more compact combustion chambers. The cars had excellent four-speed gearboxes and fully floating live axles that were extremely well made and astonishingly silent. Some models were equipped with two foot brakes. Care and caution were the chauffeur's watchwords, and needless to say, Delaunay-Bellevilles were generally chauffeur driven—at the least, Boutet de Monvel would have wanted them to be.

"You, sir," he wrote, addressing an unseen lord of

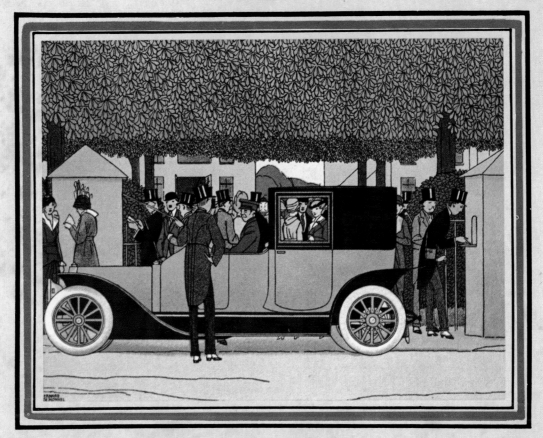

the manor, "being of the French race, know the correct usage of things and are naturally inclined toward harmonious tastes of just proportions and toward the charm of discreet colors. As for your car—I can see it as if you already had it—it will be of a shade and color that are in the pure tradition of exemplary sobriety. It will have impeccable lines, a distinction of native graciousness—like your chauffeur and footman who are always well turned out when they appear on the seat of your two-horse carriage.

". . . I firmly believe that among a hundred well-dressed women, one could easily spot a Frenchwoman. The same is true of your automobile . . . Certainly your automobile will have this allure, this body, this . . . but the name that I wish to pronounce is already on your lips. Sir, I have nothing further to point out to you. You know it just as I do." True to his word, Boutet de Monvel withheld the name of the car from his entire preface!

Charles F. Kane

A TOWN CAR TRADITION

The first examples of an expected one hundred LTD Town Cars have begun rolling out of the Dearborn shops of Andy Hotton, presumably as a test for the Ford Motor Company's approach to what has or may become the modern executive's conveyance of necessity—a reasonably priced, chauffeur-driven motorcar. Hotton, a onetime Ford executive trainee and now president of Andrew L. Hotton Enterprises, whose thirteen different companies incorporate at least that many varied aspects of the motor industry, has embarked on this new project with enthusiasm. He theorizes that his type of limousine is but one step up from Ford's present luxurious, top-of-the-line, four-door Ford Galaxy 500 LTD, and his thinking is not unrealistic.

The LTD series has substantially increased Ford's share of the luxury car market. Within the Ford line, the new LTD alone accounts for over seventeen per cent of the standard-size Ford volume and has moved the series into the luxury car position dominated for years by Chevrolet. An improved suspension system combining a unit-structured steel body with a torque box frame, coil springs and increased soundproofing have made the 1965 Fords quieter than ever, a feat that has led agency ad men to place Ford cars on a par—in this area at least—with a motorcar whose very name means luxury. There need be no comment as to the cleverness, wisdom and/or tedium of that particular campaign. Comparisons aside, the four-door LTD is a car in the American vein of luxury; its fabrics and interior trim compete respectably with customized limousine interiors. There is a choice of four different engines, including a 427-cubic-inch, 425-horsepower V-8 unit that should satisfy the most discriminating long-distance chauffeur motorcar owner. Also available on the LTD are four

different transmissions and five rear-axle ratios in specified combinations.

The overall luxury of the four-door LTD gave rise to an idea by Hotton to stretch the car a little and turn it into an economical, well-executed limousine or town car. Since the close of World War II Hotton has launched myriad automotive companies whose products range from plastic covers for automotive tools to special-bodied sports cars and whose services run the gamut from the preparation of stock cars for racing to the restoration of classic cars. Hotton's personal affection for classic cars is shown by his large collection of classic vehicles, including limousines, and his position as president of the Lincoln Owners Club. This range of experience is admirably revealed in his latest project.

Upon delivery of an LTD, whose frame has been swapped during the assembly-line process for the more rigid and heavier convertible frame, Hotton slices down through the top to extend the car a little more than two feet. A center pillar is added between the doors with a glass extension melded into the roof line. The back door is hung on the pillar, necessitating an additional rear doorpost which is welded into the door frame and top. For additional strength and rigidity, the two rear doorposts on each side are cross braced and boxed up to the roof. The center post is similarly boxed and neatly accommodates rear seat heaters. New floor pans are stamped from Kirksite dies, and a new top piece is cut, spliced, welded, filled and covered with cobra or pebble grained vinyl. Two comfortable jump seats are added to the commodious rear passenger interior area. With the addition of a glass partition, which is optional, the town car is converted into a true limousine.

Without plodding through a maze of ever-changing definitions, a limou-sine in today's terminology is a chauffeur-driven motorcar sectioned for privacy by a glass partition between the driver and passengers. The chauffeur in a limousine is provided the same privileged protection against the elements as are passengers. A town car is best described as a chauffeur-driven motorcar for business or personal transportation within a limited locality. While the chauffeur is not formally isolated by a glass barrier in the town car, the degree of protection afforded him varies according to the model year and coachmaker. In contrast, according to the prevailing definition today, the brougham places the chauffeur in a consistently vulnerable position, his only protection being a leather or cloth canopy. The brougham's usage is obviously limited and seasonable. The comparative comfort and isolation of the driver would thus appear to be the defining differences among the three styles, but unfortunately, contemporary usage finds the labels attached somewhat indiscriminantly to a variety of large, luxury vehicles, therefore antiquating even contemporary definitions.

Without further recourse to definition, it can be said that Hotton has produced a town car that is *not* what most custom-converted limousines of today have become—overstuffed, overweight and overpriced, elongated versions of standard production cars that bear striking resemblance to the ubiquitous airport limousine. The clean, simple, straight-through body lines and evenness of styling enable the LTD to be lengthened with a mini-

In 1910 this Model T Town Car sold for $1,200, including three oil lamps, a horn and tools. In addition to its liveried appeal for the elite, the Ford Motor Company suggested this model as "a splendid taxicab proposition."

mum of coachwork and interior trim, and without disturbing the car's overall balance.

A potential market for this town car or limousine is the growing number of conservative VIP's, corporate executives and government officials who take a cautious view of ostentatiously spending tax dollars, stockholders' equity or their own companies' funds to purchase what much of the general public regards as calling cars of pretentiousness. Depending upon options, engines and so forth, the approximate cost of the LTD Town Car would be seventy-five hundred dollars.

If the test proves successful and the cars are produced in quantity, the Ford Motor Company will be continuing in the town car tradition established with the Model T. In 1909 Ford brought out its first Model T Town Car, which according to later Ford literature, was the pioneer member of the Ford enclosed car family. Indeed in 1910 the Ford sales approach was directed toward this feature, the company suggesting the Town Car for winter driving rather than "getting wet and cold, walking to and waiting for a trolley car, and then standing up in the crowded car on the wet floor while the cold breezes chase the dangerous chills up and down your back every time the door opens." Within two years, however, the company slanted its sales approach to economic luxury: "the cost of this car plus the wages of a driver for two years, plus the cost of maintenance for the same period, will total less than the purchase price of the usual type of limousine." Implicit in this was the assumption that the Model T would perform equally as well as the average limousine. Special-bodied Model T town cars were made available to Ford dealers until 1918. Their selling price was generally just fifty to one hundred and

fifty dollars more than the T coupé, or about $1,000 in 1909 and $595 in 1917. When the Model A was launched in 1928, the plans included a revival of the town car idea, and special bodies were made both by the Murray and Briggs body companies in such intriguing color combinations as Madras carbuncle with a Casino red stripe, Brewster green with a Serpent green stripe and Thorne brown with an orange stripe. Unfortunately, the Model A Town Car lacked the Model T's air of jaunty dignity and was discontinued in 1930.

This latest revival of a Ford tradition could become a trend setter in the industry. It is apparent that in today's affluent society there is a demand for a chauffeured motorcar realistically priced and tastefully executed on a standard production car. That this new attempt to revive the Ford town car is based on the LTD is fortunate; few cars, if any, can be as tastefully converted.

As to the eventual success or failure of the town car test, that will have to be a wait-and-see game. The net effort will not have been lost, however, as more than one Ford official and hundreds of visitors at the Chicago show where the LTD Town Car was introduced, have exclaimed, "Here at last is a roomy, seven-passenger sedan for the good, old-fashioned, one-car, large-family man!"

—Douglas Whitfield

Less than 2,000 Model A Town Cars were produced. All were built in the style of this 1929 car and sold for $1,200. Few remain today. Both the Model A and T Town Cars are from the collection of Richard E. Williams.

COMMENTS

In presenting the history of the automobile, our editors are brought face to face with the constant need to discriminate not only between what is true and false but between what is probable and improbable as well. The past is more than the stark black and white of inalterable fact; there looms always that vague area of historical gray. For this reason decisions have to be made with a combination of knowledge, study, skepticism, common sense and intelligent presumption. New research and new interpretation can frequently reappraise or correct the judgment of historians in the past.

No history of any field is error-free. Napoleon's dictum—that history is but a fable agreed upon—perhaps crudely reveals the distrust a cursory glance at the recorded past may breed. But if historical knowledge seems less perfect than other forms of knowledge, it is the result of two human factors: the historian's personal and vicarious approach to an event that has happened and his dependence upon the veracity of data available to him. The blurred memory of an individual interviewed, the previous misinterpretation of fact, the uncorrected typographical error, the complete loss of records—all these are factors with which most historians must at some time contend.

Few publications are bereft of error, misprint, typographical flaw or omission of a fact that arrived too late. Sometimes the error is obvious, sometimes not. In either case we keenly feel it should be rectified. The correction of errors is a responsibility we owe our readers, of course. But a greater responsibility we believe is due the future automotive historian who may one day be turning our pages in quest of facts. AUTOMOBILE *Quarterly's* forthcoming four-year cumulative index will be compiled in such a manner as to single out and correct errors that have appeared in our pages. This would be an onerous, if not impossible, task were it not for the interest of our readers who take time not only to correct but to illuminate and develop unknown and unrecorded facts in relation to stories appearing in our issues. Criticisms and corrections from readers are as welcomed by us as are praise and recommendations.

The role of our editors and certainly that of our research associates is to eradicate the errors of history before press time. In this endeavor we are indebted not only to our staff of international professional historians but also to the amateurs whose assistance in the preparation of stories in their specialized area of knowledge is indispensable. Beginning with this issue, the consultants who assist us in researching individual articles will be credited in the magazine.

An unsung but invaluable consultant for our past issues has been Conte Giacinto Corte di Montonaro of Turin. The genius of the historian lies in his judgment, and we have stood in respect of Conte Corte's judgments, his criticisms, advice and his warm personal devotion to the history of the automobile. His untimely death last January was a shock to all who knew him. He was one of the first automotive historians to be officially associated with our publication when it was launched nearly four years ago.

Conte Corte, a member of the staff of the Associazione Nazionale fra Industrie Automoblistiche from 1949 to 1960, had since the mid-Fifties dedicated much of his time and enthusiasm to assisting Conte Carlo Biscaretti in the building of the Museo dell'Automobile in Turin. When the museum was opened in 1960, he resigned his ANFIA position in order to devote all his efforts to the museum and to automotive history. The Historical and Technical Documentation Center was in his charge, and in five years he amassed an impressive research library staffed by automotive researchers and linguists dedicated to keeping "the history of the motorcar always fresh for the future." His work was an inspiration to us all.

L. Scott Bailey

CONTRIBUTORS

A man whose career has ranged from the preservation of historical vehicles to the design of new ones, MAX J. B. RAUCK was born and educated in Munich, Germany. Joining Daimler-Benz in 1932, he was first a designer in the chassis building section, and he later transferred to the aircraft engine department. His natural technical-historical inclinations led to his commission by Daimler-Benz to create the historical archives of the company, a project largely destroyed by the war. In 1946 he was appointed curator of the land transportation department of the Deutsches Museum von Meisterwerken der Naturwissenschaft and Technik, Germany's national technical museum in Munich. The technical expert for the Allgemeiner Schnauferl-Club, whose history dates back to 1900, Rauck was among the organizers in 1956 of the first German veteran car rally.

Journalism, engineering and racing—each of these fields has been successfully pursued by PAUL FRÈRE. A native of France and now resident of Belgium, he spent six years in automotive engineering before leaving in 1952 to devote full-time to automotive journalism. The following year he was awarded the prize of the French Sté. des Ingénieurs de l'Automobile for the best technical article submitted by a professional journalist. The winning article dealt with modern racing car design, an area in which the author's experience had been first hand. Frère's racing career—pursued only as a sideline—began at the close of World War II with sports cars. In 1952 he graduated to the single seaters and drove on a part-time basis for the official factory teams of HWM, Gordini and Ferrari. He took second in the 1956 Belgian Grand Prix with a works Lancia-Ferrari V-8 and won the 1960 South African GP on a Cooper-Climax. In sports car races his wins include Le Mans in 1960 and Rheims in 1957 and 1958.

Born in Turin, Italy, in 1929, GIANNI ROGLIATTI traveled to Argentina as a teenager, received a degree in engineering and began his automotive career in Buenos Aires. While director of a repair shop there, he built a prototype for a two-seater sports car using the rear-mounted, two-stroke DKW engine. His journalistic career began in 1951 with an Argentinian magazine. Subsequent contributions to Italian newspapers and magazines led to his return to his native land in 1960. Currently technical editor of Italy's leading weekly car magazine *L'Automobile*, he serves also as Italian correspondent for *Autocar*, European correspondent for the Argentinian magazine *Parabrisas* and as a regular contributor of automotive articles to *La Stampa* of Turin, Italy's second largest newspaper. Because of his interest in and knowledge of automotive history, Rogliatti was recently appointed to the advisory council of the Museo dell'Automobile Carlo Biscaretti di Ruffia.

Known to many as "Mr. Sebring," ALEC ULMANN has probably contributed as much to American road racing as any of the sport's enthusiasts. Born in Russia and educated in Switzerland and America, he graduated with a degree in aero engineering, and his career was launched in that field. But his love of motor sport—which had been nurtured in Imperialist Russia by his enthusiasm for the St. Petersburg-Moscow road race of 1909—was too ardent to be quelled. In the Thirties he was instrumental in organizing the Automobile Racing Club of America, a group dedicated to reviving road racing in this country. After the war Ulmann became more devoted than ever to the idea of having racing cars in America lap something other than ovals. The original Watkins Glen, Bridgehampton, Westhampton and Floyd Bennett events were his projects. But the acme of his achievement is Sebring, which he has directed for fifteen years. The Sebring race was accepted in 1956 as a part of the World Championship series, and it has since become an American racing institution.

NOTES AND PICTURE CREDITS

CONTENTS PAGE
Illustration from the collection of Henry Austin Clark, Jr.

THE CARS OF TONY LAGO
RESEARCH CONSULTANTS: James Allward, President, Antique and Classic Car Club of Canada; Maurice Henry, Editor, *L'Équipe* of Paris; Vojta F. Mashek; Gianni Rogliatti.

THE "A" WAS FOR EVERYTHING
15, 17, 21: Photographs by Charles Miller. 14, 22 upper left: Photographs courtesy of Tory House. 18 lower right: Photograph by Herbert Sculnick. 18 upper left, 22 lower left and upper right: Photographs by Carl Malotka. Model A Ford Club of America, Inc., James Reyner, editor, Box 3433, Long Beach 3, California. Model A Restorers Club, Inc., P. O. Box 1930A, Dearborn, Michigan. RESEARCH CONSULTANTS: Leslie R. Henry, Curator, The Henry Ford Museum, Dearborn, Michigan; Sidney Strong, Executive Director, Early American Museum, Silver Springs, Florida.

ANCESTORS OF THE AUTOMOBILE
Illustrations made available to AUTOMOBILE *Quarterly* by the author. The illustrations on pages 30 and 31 were redrawn from the originals by Robert F. Andrews.

FLAWS IN THE NEW FORMULA ONE
RESEARCH CONSULTANT: Jan P. Norbye.

EPITAPH FOR THE TIN GOOSE
56: Photographs by Tom Burnside. 63: Engine photograph courtesy of Dan S. Leabu, interior photograph courtesy of Pettit's Museum of Motoring Memories. 6̄1, 62, 67: Photographs and drawings courtesy of Alex Tremulis. Tucker automobiles are on display at Pettit's Museum of Motoring Memories, Natural Bridge, Virginia; The Henry Ford Museum, Dearborn, Michigan; Harrah's Automobile Collection, Reno, Nevada. RESEARCH CONSULTANTS: William B. Hamlin, Ben Parsons.

THE KNIGHT
Photographs by Julius Weitmann.

COLIN CHAPMAN
88: Photograph by Dr. Benno Müller. 89 left, 90, 91, 92 right, 93 left: Photographs courtesy of David Phipps. 89 right: Photograph by Geoffrey Goddard. 94, 95: Photographs courtesy of Cox & Pulver, Inc., East Coast distributors of Lotus cars.

A GRAND PRIX FOR CENTRAL PARK
Drawing by Bob Shein. Map and photograph courtesy of the New York City Dept. of Parks.

DELAUNAY-BELLEVILLE
Catalogue, translated by Daphne Davis, from the collection of Robert M. Johnston, Capetown, South Africa.

A TOWN CAR TRADITION
105: Photographs by John Wisner. 107, 109: Photographs by Charles Miller.

OVERLEAF
From *The Triumph of Maximilian I*, Dover Publications, Inc., New York City.

ERRATA: Volume III, Number 2, page 176, column two, line one, for "In June of 1939, . . ." read "In June of 1938 . . ." Volume III, Number 4, page 414 and 417 caption, De Dion rear suspension was introduced in 1900, not 1896 as noted; page 414 Emile Levassor, not Constantin Krebs, designed the 1894 Panhard.

Proof sheets—suitable for framing—of individual prints, paintings and photographs appearing in color in this issue are available for purchase. A special set of seven Walter Gotschke paintings is available for $4.50. Check the tipped-in Book Society brochure for ordering information.

e believed that "whoever prepares no memorial for himself during his lifetime has none after his death." And thus in 1512, seven years before his death, Maximilian I commissioned a memorial to his reign as emperor of the Holy Roman Empire. The memorial, a series of 137 woodcuts by Germany's foremost graphic artists, is a vast triumphal procession of ornately costumed horsemen and fancifully self-propelled wagons. The wagon shown here, said to be the work of Hans Springinklee, is not unlike some of the "manumotive" vehicles described at length in the article "Ancestors of the Automobile" that appears in this issue.